CW00945174

ROUND ABOUT COLCHESTER

A view along East Street towards the town centre, 2006. The Author

ROUND ABOUT COLCHESTER

EXPLORING LOCAL HISTORY WITH THE EAST ANGLIAN DAILY TIMES

PATRICK DENNEY

Wharncliffe Books

For my grandchildren
Joseph
Jessica and Anna

First Published in Great Britain in 2006 by
Pen & Sword Wharncliffe Books
an imprint of
Pen & Sword Books Ltd
47 Church Street
Barnsley
South Yorkshire
S70 2AS

ISBN: 1 845630 05 X

A CIP catalogue record for this book is available from the British Library.

Typeset in 11/13pt Ehrhardt by Concept, Huddersfield.

Printed and bound in England by
CPI UK

Pen and Sword Books Ltd incorporates the Imprints of Pen & Sword Aviation, Pen & Sword Maritime,
Pen & Sword Military, Wharncliffe Books,
Pen & Sword Select, Pen and Sword Military Classics
and Leo Cooper.

For a complete list of Pen & Sword titles please contact
PEN & SWORD BOOKS LIMITED
47 Church Street
Barnsley
South Yorkshire
S70 2AS
England
E-mail: enquiries@pen-and-sword.co.uk
Website: www.pen-and-sword.co.uk

Contents

Foreword by Bob Russell MP

Patrick Denney has the ability to make history come alive. Readers of his articles, as recorded by him in the *East Anglian Daily Times*, already appreciate his research and revelations of events of life in and around Colchester from a bygone age – what makes his accounts so special is the blending of facts with the words of those who were there at the time.

In his latest book, appropriately titled *Round About Colchester*, Patrick Denney combines a selection of these articles in a single volume. It makes a wonderful read. Minor local events are treated with the same detailed attention as those of a more major nature.

Each section of each chapter is self-contained. There are some wonderful accounts, with people 'who were there' recalling them many years later as if they had happened only the day before.

This book is a must for anybody who has an interest in the history of Britain's Oldest Recorded Town, or who has a general interest in the social life of times not that far back.

Patrick Denney is to be commended for his dedication and commitment to recording the history of Colchester and the surrounding areas. It is his coverage of the everyday events of yesteryear alongside key occasions that make his work so rewarding and entertaining in equal measure.

The hope is that he will continue with his research into more accounts of events from the past, and that we can look forward to further articles in the *East Anglian Daily Times* and books as good as this one.

Colchester owes a debt of gratitude to Patrick Denney.

Introduction

This present collection of historical essays first saw the light of day as part of a series of local history articles published in the *East Anglian Daily Times*. They appeared as double-page features and reported on a wide range of local issues and items of historical interest. The original concept of the series, which had its first airing in the spring of 2001, had been to report on local events which were considered both newsworthy and of a kind that could be framed within an historical setting.

As far as the subject matter was concerned, there was no overriding theme, or constraints, other than the need to concentrate on Essex as a geographical setting and, in particular, on Colchester and the north of the county. And so within this general framework a wide variety of topics were explored, and those which featured Colchester and the surrounding district have been specially selected for this composition. They include stories of local buildings, anniversaries, celebrations, disasters, social events and war-time heroics. In fact, anything of a local interest that was deemed to make a good story.

In many cases the articles have featured real life accounts from people whose own memories have added a distinct flavour and reality to the past. We have, for example, received first-hand accounts of the 1953 floods, Edwardian schooldays, horse-drawn carriages, trams and numerous other personal anecdotes from the past. Other accounts have concentrated on more modern times and have featured local traders as well as individuals and groups whose actions have struck a chord in the local community.

After nearly five years of writing, the articles have grown into a compendium of local history – a kind of local history handbook – which provides a fascinating insight into local and community life. As far as the original text is concerned, only minor editing has been necessary for this volume. Likewise, most of the original illustrations that supported the text have been retained and, in some cases, complemented with fresh material. The only significant change to the whole arrangement is the way in which the material is now presented in thematic groupings, rather than in the original date order of publication.

Patrick Denney
March 2006

Acknowledgements

I am indebted to a number of people who have provided valued help and assistance in bringing this book to fruition. To begin, I would like to thank the *East Anglian Daily Times* for engaging me to write their local history column in the first place and, in particular, to Sharon Asplin who was a key figure in this regard. Other *East Anglian* staff deserving of a special mention include Julian Ford (Features Editor) and Tessa Oxlade (Picture Librarian), both of whom have generously given of their time in support of the project. And, of course, I must not forget the photographic team, including Clifford Hicks, Nick Srugnell and James Fletcher, who were responsible for taking many of the original photographs which accompanied the text in its original format.

A special word of thanks is also due to my publishers (Wharncliffe Books) for their help in formulating the idea of the book and, in particular, to Rupert Harding (Commissioning Editor), for his valued help and suggestions along the way.

My thanks is also due to Bob Russell MP for his ongoing support of the column in the *East Anglian Daily Times*, and for agreeing to add a few words of his own by way of a foreword to the book.

Finally, I would also like to thank the following organisations and individuals who have each provided me with valued assistance by way of factual information, illustrations or editorial suggestions. The list, however, does not take into account the large number of individuals who are already mentioned in the text and whose help and assistance in the project goes without saying: BGP, Colchester Borough Council, Colchester Civic Society, Colchester Local Studies Library (all staff), Colchester Museums, Colchester Zoo, Fingringhoe Historical Recorders Group, Fordham Local History Society, Mercury Theatre, St George's Junior School, Daphne Allen, Jean Blowers, Graham Bober, Peter Evans, Graham Fisher, Janet Fulford, Pam Harris, Roger Harvey, Anthony Houghton, Glen Jackson, Prue James, Jess Jephcott, David Jones, Mary Jones, Tony Petter, Andrew Phillips, Paul Taylor and Tom Wiseman.

If there are any omissions, it is with regret, and in no way intentional.

CHAPTER 1

PEOPLE

Mayor's Role is Filled with Echoes from the Past

In the summer of 2002, repeated speculation in the local press concerning the long term future of Colchester's mayor brought about an angry reaction from some quarters – almost one of disbelief. How could a town with such a rich history as Colchester even consider such a prospect, many were saying. The truth, of course, was that the town was never really in danger of losing its mayor, and the notion was merely one of many cost-saving suggestions being considered. However, it did prompt many to ask about the current role of the town's mayor and, indeed, something of the history associated with the position.

A good place to start such an investigation is by taking a stroll through the Town Hall corridors where you will be confronted with no less than 131 portraits of former town mayors gazing down from the walls (2006). The earliest is that of Roger Nunn, who first served as mayor in 1834–35, and the most recent is Terry Sutton who has just completed his term of office (May 2006). However, the position of mayor is much older than this and dates from 1635, when a charter of Charles I substituted a mayor for the previously chosen bailiffs.

Roger Nunn (the earliest mayor on show in the Town Hall) was mayor in 1834–35 and 1842–43.
East Anglian Daily Times (hereafter EADT)

The way in which an individual is chosen to become mayor has varied considerably over the years. In former times it had much to do with the status of the person concerned and the political advantage of the ruling party. For example, during a forty-two year period from 1837–1878, when the Conservative Party held political ascendancy, each and every incoming

Councillor Catherine Buchanan Alderton – the first woman mayor of Colchester, 1923–24. EADT

mayor was a Conservative candidate. From the late nineteenth century, however, and particularly from the 1920s, a much fairer system has been in place which was intended to work for the benefit of the three main parties. Nowadays, an even more amicable arrangement operates – based largely upon seniority – but also upon a fairly strict party by party rotational system.

Once decided upon, the person elected first serves as deputy mayor for a year before being officially sworn in at a special mayor-making ceremony. This takes place during May each year in the Moot Hall where the swearing of the oath of office is administered by the Town Clerk. The Town Serjeant then places the chains of office on the shoulders of both the incoming mayor and their consort.

The mayor's official chain of office is made of gold and comprises 506 links on six separate chains each of diminishing length. The chain was originally presented to the Mayor of Colchester in 1765 by a London merchant. Stories abound that in former times links of the chain would be systematically removed by successive mayors and placed on their watch chains as keep-sakes or souvenirs of their period in office. Whether this was actually the case is not known, nor indeed can it be confirmed that all the current links on the chain are original. What is apparent, however, is that the chain is extremely delicate and has actually been known to fall apart in places whilst being worn. In fact, one former mayor of fairly recent times has even admitted to substituting the entire chain whilst performing some of his various functions with a lookalike brass lavatory chain – and no-one noticed.

In addition to the chain of office, the mayor also wears a silver gilt badge which dates from 1935 and is a copy of a fifteenth century borough seal. The mayor's former badge, which was struck to commemorate Queen Victoria's Golden Jubilee in 1887, is now worn by the deputy mayor. The final parts of the mayor's appendages are made up of a black gown, with gold trimmings, and an impressive looking gold-rimmed black hat. The gown itself is something of a departure from the traditional scarlet coloured gowns worn by many other mayors and was apparently introduced at the time of Queen Victoria's funeral in 1901 and has remained ever since.

So what does the mayor actually do during his or her year-long term of office and what is the extent of their authority over political affairs? First and foremost, the mayor is the chief citizen of the town and represents the borough throughout his or her term of office. The list of official engagements which they may be expected to attend can be as many as 800–900, which averages out at between two and three for each day of the year! Although a car is provided to ferry them around, it must be an exhausting experience.

A small number of these engagements are of a mandatory nature including the opening of the Oyster Fishery, the Oyster Feast, the Freeman's Ceremony and the St George's Day Parade. But by far the majority of functions and events attended are in connection with numerous local groups and charities who regard it as a privilege to have the mayor present. At most of these events the mayor will be expected to say a few words of thanks or encouragement, and so by the end of the year should have become quite adept at public speaking, even if this was not the case previously! When attending official council meetings, the mayor acts as chairman of the council, adopting a strictly neutral, non-political stance. But like any other chairmen they do have the right to cast a deciding vote should a stalemate

Former mayors (from left) Aldeman Janet Fulford, Alderman Graham Bober and Bob Russell, Liberal Democrat MP for Colchester, on the stairs of the Town Hall with photographs of mayors from past years. EADT

The present mayor (2005–06), Councillor Terry Sutton. The Author

be reached on a particular issue. Even then, they would be expected to put aside any personal interests and opt for the status quo.

Finally, each incoming mayor chooses a theme that reflects a personal interest to run throughout their term of office. For example, in 2005–06 Terry Sutton decided upon 'Our Youth, Their Future' as his theme for the year. The mayor will also support a number of charities to benefit from any monies raised or collected during the year.

And yes, of course, it does cost the town a certain amount from public funds to support the position of mayor and the various functions related to the office. But the actual cost per head of population is relatively small, amounting to just a few pence each year. When this is compared to the value and prestige that the office brings to the town, not forgetting the sheer enjoyment experienced by countless individuals throughout the year – I, for one, think that it is money well spent.

Rooting Out Your Family's History

Researching family history is considered to be one of the fastest growing leisure activities in the UK. It is also reckoned to be the second most popular reason why people log onto the world-wide web. So why this enormous interest in family history? What draws people from all walks of life to spend much of their leisure time pouring over old documents in the local library or record office, or perhaps traipsing around overgrown churchyards in an attempt to locate a family tombstone?

For most people it is probably nothing more than an innate desire to know something about their roots and how their ancestors lived their lives. An analogy has also been made between researching family history and the reading of an historical novel. The difference for the family historian is that the central characters of the story are not merely fictitious re-creations but rather their own ancestors, who take on the role of real life individuals as the drama unfolds.

Students enrolled on a Family History class at Walton Library. The Author

Obviously carrying out such research will take time and patience, but for those with the will and determination to succeed the rewards can be most gratifying. You may, for example, end up creating a family tree stretching back several centuries and identifying forebears who were personally involved in a number of historic events. For example, you may learn of an ancestor who fought alongside Nelson at the Battle of Trafalgar, or perhaps played an active part in the English Civil War. Your ancestors may have been rich or poor, or perhaps even related to royalty. You may even, with a bit of luck, be able to trace your lineage back to the time of William the Conqueror.

But before any of this can happen, you will need to embark upon a systematic examination of available documentary sources and other related evidence. A good starting point in this regard, and one that most people tend to plump for, is an examination of

Essex Record Office archivist (Colchester branch) Paul Coverley searches for some documents in the archive storage area. The Author

Karen Sinclair and Terence Starling searching through parish registers at the Colchester branch of the Essex Record Office. The Author

the census enumerators' returns. These are the results of national surveys of the entire population which have been carried out at ten year intervals (except 1941) since 1801, although it is only from 1841 that the records are likely to contain information of a personal nature relating to your ancestors. The contents of each survey are also subject to a hundred-year closure period, so that at the present time the latest census records available for public scrutiny were those compiled in 1901. The information contained in the returns will include the name of every individual who was living in a particular place on the night of the census, along with details concerning their marital status, age, occupation and, of particular importance, where they were born. This last piece of information can be particularly valuable because knowing where a person was born can, hopefully, lead you on to locating their baptism and, in turn, the name of their parents. The exact place of birth is given from the 1851 returns onwards.

In most cases the census records are made available in the form of microfiche, or microfilm, which can usually be accessed at the local library or record office. However, each area or county will often only provide access to records pertaining to their own location, and should you wish to examine the records from places further afield you will either have to travel to that area or, instead, to the Family Records Centre in London, which holds the census records for the entire country. As a matter of interest, and for the first time ever, the 1901 census which was made public at the beginning of January 2002, was also made available on-line via the internet. Unfortunately, the operation was fraught with problems, mainly caused by the sheer number of people worldwide who attempted to log onto the site at the same time, causing it to crash. However, despite these teething problems, all now appears to be working satisfactorily. The benefit of having the records available on-line means that you are now able to search for individuals, and places, at the mere touch of a button, which can be extremely useful if you are not sure of where a particular individual or family was living at the time.

By way of an experiment, and in order to test the efficiency of the system, I decided to type in the name Charles Chaplin and a few seconds later was confronted with 151 matches.

Scrolling through the names listed I quickly identified a certain Charles Chaplin who, at the age of 12, was living in Lambeth and described as a Music Hall Artiste. I also typed in the words 'Windsor Castle' under the search for an institution section and was confronted with a list of people who were resident in the royal household at the time. At the top of the list was Edward VII, aged fifty-nine, whose occupation was simply given as 'The King', followed by sixteen-year-old Edward of Cornwall and York, who later became Edward VIII (the King's wife, Alexandra, was apparently not in residence). Although there is no charge levied to make an initial search for an individual through the indexes, you are required to pay a small fee if you decide that you would like some further information, or perhaps wish to view and download a copy of the original census page.

The census is of course just one of many sources available that you may be able to gain information from. Parish registers, that is records of baptisms, marriages and burials, could possibly help you to trace an individual back over 400 years if you are lucky, and indeed if the records have survived. Then there are numerous maps, wills, deeds, rate books, directories, poor law accounts, taxation records, tithe records, manorial records and so the list goes on. But bear in mind that most of the information that you will find will be fragmentary in form and you will need painstakingly to piece it all together, in much the same way as you might complete a jigsaw puzzle – although with a jigsaw one normally has access to all the pieces available before you start and you also have a pretty good idea of what the end result should look like – not the case, I'm afraid with family history research!

Julia Goodbourn receives advice from Colchester Local Studies librarian Richard Shackle. The Author

One person who has recently been bitten by family history bug is Julia Goodbourn, who lives with her husband and two children at Stoke-by-Nayland. Julia recalls that despite having had an interest in her family history for the last twenty or so years, it is only in recent months that she has finally found the time to do something about it:

> I have always been fascinated by family history and looking at old photographs, and wondering where all these people fitted in, and this is the first opportunity that I've had to spend some time to carry out some research. The problem was that I didn't know how to set about the research and when I heard about a University of Essex family history course taking place, decided to join. It was absolutely ideal because it has set me on the right track. Before the course started I had done no research at all, but I have since been able to trace my family back a further four generations. I've used the census, both on-line and microfiche, parish registers, various web-sites and I'm planning to look at some wills. I've found marriages between first cousins, deaths, gravestones and even details about a relative who died in the First World War, and where he is buried. I just find the whole thing so fascinating.

From speaking with a relative beginner, I then turned my attention to someone whose interest in family history was originally fostered as a small child some sixty years ago. William Wild, who lives at Thorrington, is a seasoned family historian with a wealth of knowledge about his family's origins and the sources that have yielded that information:

> My father was deeply interested in family history so I was sort of immersed in it from a youngster. I must confess, however, that when your father is so interested in something and tends to ram it down your throat, you tend to switch off a bit. And it was only when he died about 15 years ago that I really became interested again. We were fortunate in the fact that our family lived on the same farm for about 300 years and they accumulated a mass of documents which ultimately passed down to my father and then onto me. The collection contains dozens of manorial records, indentures, leases and various other family papers. Of particular interest is a document relating to the death of my three times great aunt whose name was Martha Wild. When she was buried in 1834 her next of kin paid a third party more than £8 to keep a watch over the churchyard for forty-six nights in case her grave may have been targeted by grave robbers. I also have the undertaker's bill for the funeral, which itemises such things as the kind of gloves that the mourners had to wear, and how much they had to pay for the coaches and horses. It even states how much they had to pay at the toll house because they had to pass through the toll gate to get from one parish to another.

Despite being extremely knowledgeable on the subject, William is still attending courses on family history, and computing, on the premise that there is always something new to learn.

William Wild with a portrait of his great-grandfather, Henry James Wild, and a copy of his family tree dating back to the 1500s. The Author

William Wild with a copy of his great-grandfather's will. The Author

Part of a receipt for watching over the grave of Martha Wild for forty-six days in 1834.

Do 23 Do 17
Do 24 Do 18
Do 25 Do 19
Do 26 Do 20
Do 27 Do 21
Do 28 Do 22
Do 23
Do 24

46 Nights at 3s 6d Each Night £8..1..0
Recd of Mr John Weekley £5 -- Due £3..1..0

The Life and Times of Lucky Crick

On 20 September 1854, the British Army took part in one of the most important battles of the Crimean War when they successfully defeated the Russians at the crossing of the Alma river. The storming of the heights of the Alma has gone down in military folklore as one of the most daring actions ever embarked upon in wartime, and it set the scene for other notable actions at Sebastopol, Balaclava and Inkerman. It was fitting, therefore, that to mark the 150th anniversary of the event in October 2004, the Royal Mail issued a set of commemorative stamps depicting some of the ordinary soldiers who took part in the war. On a more local level, we decided to mark the event by relating the experience of an Essex man who was also involved in the action – and who lived to tell the tale. His name was Zachariah Crick and his proud descendants still live in the Colchester area.

Zachariah Crick was born at Bradfield in Essex in 1831 and was the second son of three born to Thomas and Milly. In addition to his two brothers, William (b.1828) and Charles (b.1832), Zachariah also had seven half-brothers and sisters from his father's first marriage to Elizabeth Gosling, who had died in 1821.

In October 1833, when Zachariah was just two years old, his father was convicted at the Essex Quarter Sessions for stealing two bushels of wheat from his master's barn at Tendring and was sentenced to seven years transportation to New South Wales. As it turned out, young Zachariah was never to see his father again as he died in Australia about half way

The family of Crimea veteran Zachariah Crick (from the left) Robert and David Crick (great-great grandsons) and Geoff Crick (great grandson) who live in Colchester. EADT

through his sentence. Back in Essex, however, his widow Milly was struggling to make ends meet and was finally compelled to abandon her two youngest sons, Zacahriah and Charles to the workhouse. Milly was subsequently prosecuted for this action, but the court apparently found it hard to decide what to do with her. As for her two young boys, it would appear that they remained in the workhouse until they were old enough to leave and find work.

After leaving the workhouse Zachariah decided to go to sea and managed to get a job on a flat-bottomed barge called the *Bramble* which was employed in transporting coal from the northern ports of England to Mistley in Essex. On his first trip between Mistley and Middlesbrough, the boat ran into a terrible storm which raged for three days and nights and from which none of the crew expected to survive. Lady luck, however, was on their side and no lives were lost. Zachariah remembered that when he arrived home on a Sunday evening, and despite being wet through to the skin, he fell onto the hearth rug and slept until the following night, despite his mother's attempts to rouse him. Zachariah refused to go to sea again, believing the boat to be unsafe, and so the Captain, Harry Corbell, took on another lad for the next voyage. The boat once again ran into a storm, but this time its bottom broke and all of the crew, except for the Captain, were drowned. Zachariah was obviously considered to be a very fortunate young man and later came to be known as 'Lucky Crick' in the Mistley and Bradfield area of Essex.

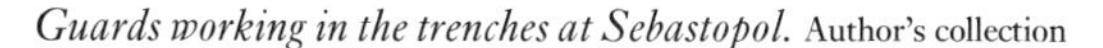

Guards working in the trenches at Sebastopol. Author's collection

At the age of 19 Zachariah decided to join the army, and on 26 April 1850 he enlisted in the Grenadier Guards, which he later declared to be the right-hand regiment of the world and a pattern for the British Army. He remained in service for ten years before retiring on a special pension of ninepence (4p) a day. During his service period, however, he saw much action and served for a time in the Crimea. He was present at the Battle of the Alma, and at the Siege of Sebastopol, when his friends to the right and left of him were killed. Zachariah only received 'a light touch', as he called it, on his left knee, but lost no duty through it. He recalled that after taking the heights of Alma from the Russians, the English soldiers were huddled together on a piece of land which was planted with onions, and that he and his comrades stuffed their haversacks full with them and later feasted on them. He also had vivid memories of the bitter cold weather during the campaign and how on the night before the battle of the Alma they had to spend the night lying out in the open under a single blanket, with no man daring to take his clothes off. Interestingly, one of his battlefield companions throughout the entire campaign was his elder half-brother Thomas Crick who may have provided the inspiration for his having joined the regiment in the first place.

Zachariah also spoke with gratitude of the kindness that was shown to him by Prince Edward of Saxe Weimar, who was in command of his company, and also by John Begoring, who was wounded in the ankle whilst carrying the colours at Alma. Zachariah's pride and joy, however, were his two campaign medals (the Crimean with two clasps and the Turkish) which he always wore with pride. He used to boast that while he may not have much gold, he would always have some silver about him, for he would never part with his treasured medals.

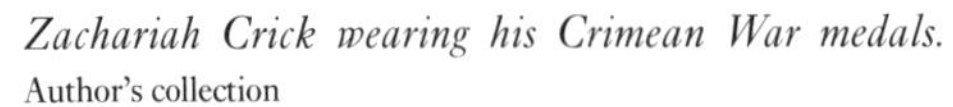
Zachariah Crick wearing his Crimean War medals.
Author's collection

Following Sebastopol, Zachariah was invalided home and was eventually discharged from the army on 28 April 1869, having completed ten years service. Just three weeks later, on 22 May 1860, he signed up with the West Riding Police Force where he remained until October 1864. Apparently, by this time, he was beginning to lose his sight and was forced to retire from duty. He had also by this time married Emma Nowell, from Pontefract, and had become father to three young children. He decided to move his family back to his home county of Essex where he found employment as a brick-maker in Kirby Cross (an occupation apparently favoured by the blind) and continued working in the industry until he retired many years later. By the 1870s he had moved his growing family to a new brickfield which had opened in the district of Old Heath at Colchester.

Zachariah with his grandson Stanley and companion parrot in the early 1900s. Author's collection

As time went on Zachariah's eyesight slowly deteriorated and by the late 1880s he had become totally blind. He was still, however, working in the brickfields and would apparently travel to and from his place of work by donkey and cart, with the donkey responsible for negotiating the route! Unfortunately, his wife had also by this time become totally deaf so communication between the couple was a bit of a problem. He did, however, have a trusted companion in the form of a parrot which his son-in-law had brought back from South America. The bird was apparently a great mimic and had a large repertoire of songs, whistles and chatter which would fill a two hour programme.

One particular event that the old Guardsman used to look forward to in his later years were the occasions when HRH the Duke of Cambridge (also a Crimean veteran and first

The Duke of Cambridge and staff arriving in Colchester to inspect the garrison around 1895. Author's collection

The Duke of Cambridge, himself a veteran of the Crimea and later Commander-in-Chief of the Army. Author's collection

cousin to Queen Victoria) used to visit the town to inspect the garrison. Zachariah would join the crowds of people lining the street at the top of North Hill to stand and salute his former Commander-in-Chief, as he rode up North Hill with his staff from the railway station.

Despite his long and interesting life, and his undoubted devotion to his country, his final years were spent in fairly distressed circumstances. He only had a meagre pension to survive on and the workhouse doors were beckoning. His case was finally taken up by the Colonel Commanding the Grenadier Guards who, in 1906, secured him an additional pension of two shillings and sixpence a week from The Incorporated Soldiers and Sailors Society.

Zachariah finally passed away on 21 November 1910 in his 81st year. He was one of the last survivors of the Crimean campaign and was buried at Colchester cemetery with full military honours. Unfortunately, there were no Guards available to attend his funeral, but the day was saved by the Gordon Highlanders, who, being stationed in the town at the time, were only too happy to oblige. And so in a very solemn procession, which took place just before 3 pm on Saturday 26 November 1910, Zachariah's body was drawn through the streets of Colchester on a gun carriage as his friends and neighbours gathered to say their goodbyes.

Fighting to Preserve the Town's Finest Features

Keep up the good work – and congratulations to the Colchester Civic Society who, in 2004, celebrated forty years as the principal watchdog of the town's architectural heritage and future development. The group was founded in succession to the Colchester Preservation Society (active in the 1950s) on 24 June 1964, in response to growing concerns that the

SUCCESS: The redevelopment of Sir Isaac's Walk with traditional-style buildings is pleasing to the eye. The Author

kind of unbridled post-war development which was taking place in towns and cities throughout the country, and which was resulting in the blatant destruction of many historic town centres, could also happen here in Colchester. Developers at the time, of course, were beginning to form partnerships with local authorities for the purpose of pursuing large-scale redevelopment schemes, often with little regard for existing historic buildings and other traditional features. What was needed was a dedicated focus group who could monitor such events on the public's behalf and act as a lobby group in favour of those who supported the preservation of the town's heritage.

It is easy, of course, to be wise after the event, but with hindsight it is now clear that the 1960s proved to be a turning point in the town's history, particularly as far as its architecture was concerned. Slowly but surely Colchester was losing its cosy market town image and developing into a modern regional centre. But at what cost? Fortunately, the town's scarring by 1960s-style architecture, which was responsible for the creation of many 'concrete jungles' throughout the country, was minimal, and with the exception of a handful of glaring examples, for the most part the modern development of the town has been achieved in a manner which has resulted in an acceptable mix of old and new.

The idea of forming a new Civic Society in the town was first decided upon at a dinner party held in the *Fleece Hotel* attended by such notable figures as Ken Mabbitt, Bernard Mason, John Bensusan-Butt, Duncan Clark and Alderman Dansie, all of whom were concerned that part of the town's heritage may be at risk. The result was that a steering group was formed to examine what could be done, and to investigate what was happening with similar groups elsewhere, in the hope that something positive could also be achieved in Colchester. The findings of the report indicated that such a group would indeed be well supported and a massive leaflet drop was arranged to all the homes in the Borough informing them of a public meeting due to be held in the Town Hall for the purpose of fully debating the matter. The result was that several hundred people turned up to witness the formation of the new society and the setting up of a number of committees, each charged with a different area of expertise.

The new Society soon became active in local affairs and over the next couple of years notched up one or two notable achievements. They attended their first planning enquiry on 25 August 1965 with regard to proposed alterations to a particularly fine bow-window at Heasman and Son's shop in the High Street, and in the following January hosted the 'Brighter Streets Exhibition' in St Martin's Church. Their first major contribution to the preservation of the town's heritage, however, came a couple of years later, in December 1967, with the launch of the Scheregate Improvement Scheme. This included members having to approach all the various owners and occupiers of buildings in the area to try and persuade them to agree to adopting a similar colour scheme for their individual premises, which would be both attractive and a benefit to the whole community.

But as noted above, the Society's formative years were not without their problems as they kept an ever close watch on the new 1960s-style architecture which was beginning to sweep the country. Out went the traditional red brick and tile to be replaced with acres of

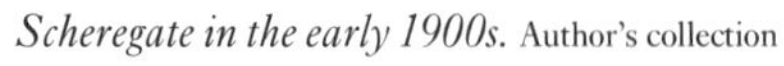

Scheregate in the early 1900s. Author's collection

SUCCESS: Scheregate still retains its old-world charm. The Author

FAILURE: The loss of the splendid red-brick fãade of the Cups Hotel *is clearly evident from these before and after views of the site.* Author's collection

Houses in the Dutch Quarter before restoration. Author's collection

SUCCESS: The regeneration of the Dutch Quarter area in the 1950s was one of the town's architectural success stories. The Author

concrete in the form of ugly square blocks, seemingly oblivious to the well-tried traditional buildings surrounding them. Perhaps the most glaring example of this in Colchester was the construction of the new Telephone Manager's Office in West Stockwell Street which raised its ugly head above the town's skyline in 1968. Despite vociferous protests from various quarters, including the Civic Society itself, building work went ahead under the cover of Crown Immunity, effectively snuffing out any attempt at compromise or negotiation. Today, the building is still viewed by many as one of the worst eyesores in the town from an architectural point of view.

Another disaster from 1968 was the loss of the famous *Cups Hotel* in the High Street with its splendid brick-fronted façade. This was the result of a property deal struck between developers and the council, and despite a determined effort by members of the Society to save the building, everyone was dismayed to find that on the morning of 6 March 1968 demolition work on the building had been taking place overnight.

Throughout the 1970s and 1980s the Society were kept extremely busy as large tracks of the town centre were completely redeveloped to form our present shopping centres at Lion Walk and Culver Square. But the group were also active in many other areas including the Cannock Mill Project, which ensured that surrounding woodland and walkways were not totally given over for housing, as well as the successful campaign to create the Roman River Valley Conservation Area.

FAILURE: The construction of the Telephone Manager's Office in West Stockwell Street did nothing to enhance the skyline of the historic town. The Author

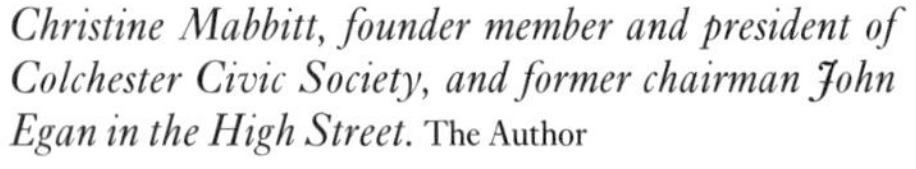

Christine Mabbitt, founder member and president of Colchester Civic Society, and former chairman John Egan in the High Street. The Author

Today the Society's work continues unabated. The St Botolph's Regeneration Scheme, the Roman Wall and major work at The Hythe are just some of the issues keeping group members busy. But as we move forward into the 21st century, the Society has found yet other issues to deal with. These are aptly described by Mrs Christine Mabbitt (President of the Society) as 'quality of life issues' and include problems associated with the large number of night-time activities in the town, as well as the rise in anti-social behaviour caused by excessive drinking. Obviously this is a trend that we should all be concerned about in order that out town centres remain safe and accessible for all.

Canterbury Tales

Towards the end of April 2003, the pupils and staff of St George's Junior School in Colchester were busy putting the finishing touches to a centenary exhibition to celebrate the founding of their school a hundred years earlier. Invitations to attend the event were extended to parents, friends and former pupils and, on the day itself, attractions included a display of school memorabilia and a selection of 1903 musical 'hits' sung by the school's centenary choir. The school is an imposing structure of red brick, typical of the period of when it was built, and with a spacious feel about it despite its restricted site in the middle of a built up housing area. In fact, despite the comings and goings of generations of local children over the intervening years, the building still appears to be in pristine condition, a testament to its Edwardian builders.

The school, which began its life in April 1903 as Canterbury Road Mixed Council School, was built as part of an ambitious school building programme which had been conceived a decade earlier. In the early 1890s, it had become apparent that the ever-increasing financial burden of maintaining adequate school accommodation in the town was proving too much for the church authorities. With a deficiency of 528 places, and a further 1,062 places far below the required standard, it was finally decided in 1892 to yield to the setting up of a school board, funded by the rates, to remedy the situation. By the turn of the century five new schools had been built to accommodate an additional 3,000 pupils. In 1902, the Balfour Education Act abolished the school boards and transferred their responsibilities to the local authorities, with the former board schools now becoming known as council schools. In Colchester the new Act took affect from 1 April 1903, with the forming of a new education committee, chaired by Alderman Wilson Marriage. The new committee continued with the old board's programme of expansion with further schools being opened at Canterbury Road in 1903, Mile End in 1906 and East Ward in 1908.

However, getting back to Canterbury Road School (its name was changed to St George's in 1953), and with the help of some surviving school records and memories of former pupils, we can now take a look back to the early years of the school's history and to life in the class-room as experienced by the some of the school's earlier pupils. The school opened on

A classroom at Canterbury Road School from around 1920. Author's collection

A view of the same classroom in 2003. David Jones

20 April 1903 with 314 pupils, who had been drawn from a number of other local schools, but predominately from St John's Green, Barrack Street and Kendall Road. The children were divided into eight classes averaging between forty and fifty in size, and were taught by an initial staff of seven teachers led by headmaster William Hodgson, who was employed on a salary of £200 a year.

After taking a few days to settle down, the headmaster recorded his first entry in the new school log book on 30 April, 1903. He wrote: 'Mrs Leech states that her daughter has had much of her own way but that with firmness on the part of the teachers she can be made to mind.' Later, in 1917, a young lad named Horace Scott was insolent to his teacher and subsequently disciplined. A follow-up letter to his father brought an apology and a request to 'break him in.' The head reported that he had been subdued and was amenable ever since.

Exactly how the teachers exercised their 'firmness' is not noted, but teachers of the period were far stricter than their modern counterparts. Punishment for misbehaviour of any kind usually came in the form of a short, sharp shock, with the use of the cane being commonplace. Former pupils recalled that if anyone misbehaved they would usually be sent to stand next to Mr Hodgson's desk, which was located at the Canterbury Road end of the upper hall. They had to stand in an area which was known as 'The Square' until the headmaster decided to deal with them. After listening to both sides of the argument, punishment, if merited, would then be metered out by either the headmaster or the teacher concerned. An amusing account in this regard was recalled by former pupil Alan Wilson who attended the school from 1915:

> I remember one boy who was sent to stand in the square. His case was heard and he was given two strokes of the cane. Mr Soar, the teacher, was told to mete out the punishment. The boy held out his hand, Mr Soar raised the cane, and then the next thing we knew was that the boy had grabbed the cane and was chasing Mr Soar around the hall.

Another somewhat humorous recollection of discipline in the classroom was recalled by Margaret Golby who first attended the school in 1906:

> I can always remember one teacher that we had there. We used to call him 'Daddy Soar', his name was Mr Soar. Well, he came round the class one day and I was sitting on the edge of the desk, and he tapped me on the top of the head and said, 'What are you sitting like that for?' And I said, 'cause that girl's got nits in her hair.' Well, if I'd have gone home with them in my hair my mother would have been upset.

A large number of entries in the log book are concerned with attendance figures, and the need to maintain high percentages of attendance. No doubt with one eye on the school's annual grant, particularly the part relating to good attendance figures, the head was quick to mitigate any low numbers with a variety of excuses including illness, children attending excursions and bad weather. In fact, on the occasion of a severe thunderstorm on 27 July

1904, the head made a point of noting the fact that he had been compelled to send sixty-six children home who were in a more or less soaked condition, and who most probably would have caught colds by being retained in school. The total number of absentees that particular day had actually been 144 so was this perhaps a early attempt at trying to bury bad news!

Again, on 4 September 1903, the head decided to close the school for the day owing to large numbers of children expected to attend Buffalo Bill's Wild West Show in the afternoon. This was an event which caused considerable excitement throughout the town for

A page from a souvenir guide purchased at Buffalo Bill's Wild West Show at Colchester in September 1903.
Anthony Houghton collection

both young and old alike. Buffalo Bill's large entourage, which included 800 performers and over 500 horses, had arrived early in the morning at North Station on three specially hired trains. Thousands of onlookers had lined the streets as the troop, which included large numbers of Sioux Indians, Plains Cowboys and Russian Cossacks, paraded their way to the show ground at Reed Hall. By mid-day a spacious arena had been erected with under-cover seating for 10,000. In the afternoon, the town almost ground to a halt as many shops and businesses closed early to allow their staff to attend. This is not to mention the thousands of schoolchildren (including those from Canterbury Road) who also flocked to the event. The assembled audience was treated to an exciting display of horsemanship and shooting, culminating with what was advertised as the greatest of living dramas – The Attack on the Deadwood Stage. The entire programme was repeated in the evening when over 8,000 people braved a severe thunderstorm to attend. By midnight, the entire camp had been dismantled and Buffalo Bill was en route to his next venue.

An entry in the log book for 25 January 1908, highlights another problem which was fairly prevalent at the time – that of ill-nourished or underfed children. The head does not elaborate on the extent of the problem but confirms that arrangements were to be made for up to thirty children from the school to be provided with a breakfast and mid-day meal. The meals were provided by the Mayor's Poor Children's Fund, with hundreds of children across the borough affected.

During the First World War, children from the school played their part in supporting the war effort by collecting horse chestnuts, the oil from which was used to help make margarine. A total of thirty bushels of horse chestnuts were subsequently collected by the children of the school. Another initiative, supported by children from most of the schools in the borough in order to protect the crops from the scourge of butterflies and caterpillars, was a scheme whereby children were paid a penny for a dozen dead butterflies. One can imagine, however, hoards of youngsters trampling over allotments and gardens with their butterfly nets swishing away, resulting in considerably more damage to the crops than the butterflies would have caused.

Former pupil John Conner, aged ninety, in 2003. EADT

Another interesting note in the log book for 19 September 1913, records the fact that the key, nail and match game has again suddenly arisen, and that the head had decided to confiscate all keys. This intriguing entry was explained by former pupil John Conner, who at the age of ninety could remember this rather dangerous pastime:

> At playtime some of the boys would get a large key and fill the inside up with the ends of some red matches. They would then ram a nail into the key which was tied to a piece of string before swinging it hard against the ground, making the mixture within explode.

John also recalled numerous other playground games including marbles, which he said they used to play in the middle of the road on the way home from school. Apparently there was little in the way of traffic to worry about apart from the odd horse and cart.

Finally, although the exterior of the school has seen little in the way of change over the years, the layout of some of the interior rooms have changed beyond recognition, particularly with regard to the seating arrangements in the classrooms. Doris Lawson (nee Humm) who at ninety-four years of age had fond memories of her ten year stint at the school:

Former pupil Doris Lawson, aged ninety-four, in 2003. EADT

> When we started in the morning we all had to march into the hall for prayers. The headmaster had a desk in there and the naughty children would have to go and stand by his desk. In the classrooms, our desks were all set out in straight rows, facing the front, with steps going up towards the back, and we had slates which were kept propped up at the front of our desks.

CHAPTER 2

PLACES

'Best House' Gives a Taste of History

The internationally-renowned historian, Nikolaus Pevsner, once described Hollytrees as 'the best 18th century house in Colchester.' Certainly the building exudes elegance, and its position at the edge of Castle Park, at very heart of an area that was once dominated by some of the town's wealthiest families and merchants further testifies to its importance in the cultural history of the town. Of course, most of us today will be more familiar with its role as a museum dedicated mainly to the home and social life of the town over the last three or so hundred years. Many will also be aware that in 2001 the building was given

Hollytrees in the early 1900s when the building was still a domestic residence. Author's collection

The front view of Hollytrees Museum. Author's collection

The front view of Hollytrees as it was in the early 1930s. Only the holly trees, planted on the right, give away its position. Many of the buildings surrounding it are long gone. Author's collection

The first known illustration of Hollytrees as it was depicted on Pryor's Prospect of Colchester *in 1724. The men in the foreground are cloth workers and the windmill is in Mersea Road.* Author's collection

a substantial makeover, which included a complete refurbishment of its displays. But more of this later – let's begin by looking back at the origins of the building.

The house was built around 1718 by Elizabeth Cornelisen, a wealthy widow, who had purchased the site from the estate of the previous owners. Unfortunately she died soon after the new building was completed and the house descended to her niece, Sara Webster, the daughter of a wealthy merchant, and who at that time was married to Ralph Creffield. The couple moved from their Ardleigh home to occupy the house which later became known as 'Creffields'. Unfortunately her husband died shortly after moving to Colchester, and Sara went on to marry Charles Gray in about 1726.

Charles Gray was a local lawyer and respected antiquarian. He was also very

One of the many interior displays showing a house servant at work in the 1840s. The Author

A penny farthing bicycle from the 1880s. The Author

much involved in local politics serving as Member of Parliament for the town in five elections. Gray apparently wasted little time in setting out to improve his house and gardens with one of his first tasks being to plant the now famous holly trees which stand at the front of the house. This act is noted in his diary where he writes: '1729 – The hollys planted in ye middle of March and grassed in ye kitchen garden.' These trees, of course, have since given rise to the current name of the house.

This purpose-built 'Hollytrees' dolls house is a popular addition to the exhibits. The Author

One of many antique children's toys on display to the public. The Author

The next major undertaking by Gray took place in 1748 when he had a new west wing added to the building. The extension was designed by local architect James Deane, and whilst adding considerably to the accommodation, it did little to maintain the building's symmetry. Gray again made reference to the building work in his diary: 'begun in Ap., finished in November, ye addition to ye house, vizt: ye servants' hall, Library and chamber over it.'

Gray lived in the house until his death in 1782 at the age of eighty-six, and following his second wife's death in 1796, the house reverted once again to the Creffield family and then to the Rounds of Birch Hall through the marriage of Tamar Creffield to James Round. The Round family were to hold the property (which incidentally came with the castle and extensive grounds) for the next 120 or so years before it was sold to Colchester Borough Council in 1922.

The 1881 census provides us with an interesting insight into the occupation of the house during the Victorian years. The head of the house at the time was James Round whose occupation is described as, 'MP & JP & Landowner'. Living with him was his wife Sibylla and their six daughters, his sister, a niece, a governess and eight servants – making a grand total of nineteen persons sharing the building – where on earth did they all sleep because the house is not that big!

End of an era: shortly after this picture was taken in May 2000, the extensive library belonging to the Essex Society for Archaeology and History was transferred from its former home in Hollytrees Museum to the University of Essex. The Author

The view from the new entrance to Hollytrees Museum in Castle Park. The Author

The sale of the property to the borough council in 1922 was aided greatly by the extreme generosity of Viscount and Viscountess Cowdray who defrayed the entire cost of the transfer. Lord Cowdray (Weetman Pearson) had previously been MP for Colchester between 1895–1910.

In 1929 the building opened as a museum of bygones from more recent times. The range of exhibits included toys, domestic and craft objects, military ephemera, costume and needlework displays. The floors above the museum area became home to the extensive library of the Essex Society for Archaeology and History, a collection which has subsequently found a new home at the University of Essex.

The programme to revamp the Museum's displays in 2000–2001 meant that the building had to be closed to the public for over a year whilst the alterations – which included the installation of a new lift – took place. The end result was an impressive range of exciting new displays designed to make the past come to life for the visitor. Concentrating mainly on our more recent past, the displays focus largely on the lives of real people with opportunities to listen to taped recordings of local residents recalling and reliving their memories, and being able to interact with a range of other related material.

A central feature on the ground floor display area is a specially commissioned doll's house which has been constructed as a scaled down model of the Hollytrees building. Each room can be explored, or played with by younger visitors, particularly as part of specially arranged school visits.

Theatre's Unique Role in the Life of a Town

The Mercury Theatre in Colchester is nearly thirty-five years old and currently enjoying something of a resurgence in popularity. Visitor numbers are high – and growing – and the theatre is rightly regarded as a major asset to the town and the surrounding area, adding enormous value to the social and cultural life of its inhabitants. But before considering life at the Mercury in more detail, what do we know of the history of theatre in Colchester generally?

The Mercury Theatre and Victorian Water Tower (Jumbo). The Author

The earliest recorded theatres in the country were those built by the Romans – and what magnificent structures they must have been. At the time of writing, only four such theatres have been discovered in Britain, two of which are in Colchester and both would have been capable of seating upwards of 3,500 people. The others are at Canterbury and St Albans.

In modern times, the earliest purpose-built theatre in Colchester was erected in 1764, by a theatre company from Norwich, on a small piece of land behind the Moot Hall. Although not grand in design, it could accommodate up to 300 people and was to serve the town's theatrical needs for a period of nearly fifty years. In 1812, a new theatre, later named the Theatre Royal, was built in Queen Street. It had seating for over a thousand and for many years was the principal place of entertainment in Colchester. From the early 1900s, however, its popularity began to wane as a result of a new variety theatre opening in the High Street which was soon to be playing to packed audiences twice nightly. The new building was later renamed the Hippodrome and went on to specialise in vaudeville and variety. Meanwhile, at the Theatre Royal, despite a period of refurbishment in 1907, audiences continued to decline, and its demise came in 1918 when the building was destroyed by fire.

The old Theatre Royal in Queen Street – the first of Colchester's modern-day theatres. Author's collection

Various other playhouses and cinemas had opened in the 1920s and 1930s, but it

was not until 1937 that the town once again had a full-time theatre. This was the result of the initiative of a man called Robert Digby, who with just a few pounds behind him had set up the Colchester Repertory Company in the old Albert Hall building in the High Street. After a faltering start the venture became something of a success, particularly during the war years, when crowds flocked to see the weekly performances. During the 1950s, however, attendances started to decline and to many the theatre was becoming something of a lost cause despite numerous injections of funding.

The problem came to a head in 1963 when Robert Digby died and a search was made for his successor. The theatre's Board of Directors advertised the position in *The Stage* and *The Guardian* and received seventy-four applications for the post. From a shortlist of just seven they began a series of interviews at their office in West Stockwell Street and the second person to be interviewed was a young man named David Forder, who was currently working the Belgrade Theatre in Coventry. Dennis Thorogood, who was sitting on the interview panel at the time, remembers that David was head and shoulders above the rest and that the committee wanted to offer him the job there and then. 'He was the only one of the seven who had taken the trouble to go to the theatre and see the production,' Dennis recalls, 'and he wasn't frightened to speak his mind.'

David Forder himself also remembers the occasion:

> The night before the interview I decided to go to the Repertory Theatre to see what it was like. So along I went from the *Cups Hotel* where I was staying and

The building on the right of this picture in Colchester High Street became the Repertory Theatre in 1937.
Author's collection

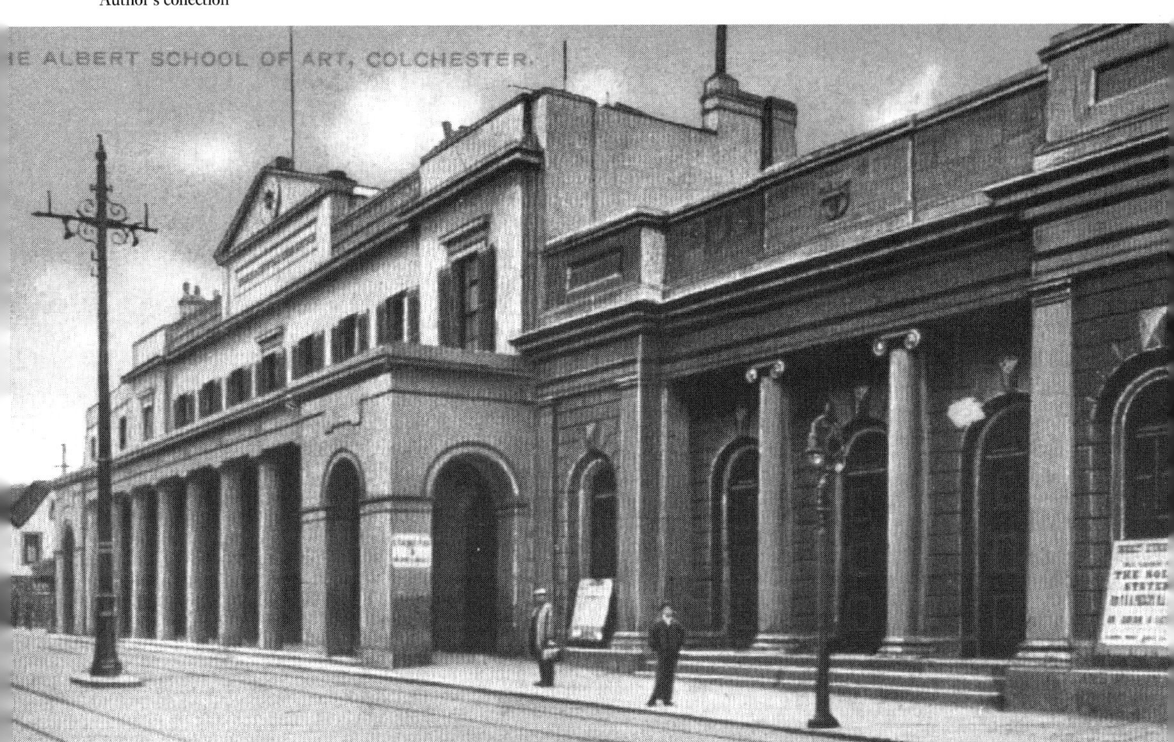

Robert Digby (third from left front row) and his company sitting outside the Repertory Theatre shortly before embarking upon a tour of British forces overseas in May 1940. Peter Evans collection

discovered that the theatre was housed in a converted art gallery, and it was pretty tumbledown – very run down indeed. And it didn't smell very nice either. Anyway, I went in. The average age of the audience was about seventy-two; the average sex of the audience was female; the average hat was hand-knitted and pulled down over the hearing aid and there was about thirty-two of them, as I counted. And the standard, well I can't describe how poor I thought it was – which surprised me because I knew the theatre had a fine history and had done some great work during the war. So I decided that it was so bad, and that I was in such a wonderful place in Coventry, that I couldn't possibly come to Colchester and I went ahead the next morning with the interview deciding that no way was I coming. I was so outspoken at the interview, to the point of being rude, telling them that unless they did something pretty quick they wouldn't last six weeks. So back to the *Cups Hotel* I went and just as I was leaving there was a message for me from the Bishop of Colchester, the Chairman of the Board of Directors, saying that he wanted to see me straight away. When I arrived on his doorstep he said to me. 'Well, I wanted someone much more exciting, but the Board has chosen you – come in.'

David Forder in 2002. EADT

This proved to be a turning point in the fortunes of the theatre, for no sooner had David arrived and confirmed his initial evaluation of things, he had set about building a new team and gradually started to pull things around. The first problem was to increase visitor numbers and this was achieved partly by taking the decision to get out into the community and promote the theatre to the general public, a notion that had not been taken up by his predecessor: 'I used to be out two or three nights a week speaking to various groups,' David recalled. 'Village halls, Women's Institutes, Young Farmers – you name it – it was really a fun evening because, having been an actor, I knew how to make people laugh, and my fee was a "coach party" booking to the theatre.'

Before long, audience numbers had doubled and things were starting to look much brighter. There was still the problem, however, of the building itself, which was totally inadequate for use as a theatre, as well as the need to secure funding from the various local and governmental authorities. So a campaign was started to galvanise public opinion of the need for a new theatre to enhance the amenities of the town. The *Essex County Standard*, under the leadership of Hervey Benham, played a crucial role in this area by running numerous features highlighting the fact that it was nothing short of a scandal that we were not getting a new theatre, and everybody who was anybody got behind the campaign.

In 1967 the Council finally agreed to support the building of a new theatre and to provide a suitable site at a peppercorn rent. A local man, Norman Downie, was appointed architect

Chief Executive Dee Evans with the cast from 'Present Laughter' and the Mercury support team in April 2002. EADT

Gregory Floy and Christine Absalom from a scene in Noel Coward's Present Laughter, *2002. Mercury Theatre*

for the new building and, together with assistance from Christopher Morley, head of design at the Royal Shakespeare Company, came up with a unique and innovative hexagonal design which was to allow the stage to be adapted for either a traditional picture-frame format, or an open stage. The target cost for the building was about £200,000, a third of which had to be raised locally from members of the public.

The new theatre finally opened on 10 May 1972 to a production of *The Recruiting Officer* which proved to be so successful that they had to stage three opening nights. The first actor to appear on the stage was Eric Porter (Soames in the *Forsyte Saga*) who delivered a prologue in a pose of a bowler-hatted Mercury, complete with winged boots!

Over thirty years on, the Mercury Theatre is still very much with us. It has, of course, had its share of ups and downs over the years, including a devastating fire in 1996 which destroyed much of the stage area, resulting in a prolonged period of closure. Even after reopening some months later it took a while for visitor numbers to return to previous levels, and securing financial support has been an ongoing problem. But things do now appear to be on the up and up once again, particularly since the appointment in 1998 of Dee Evans as Chief Executive. Dee, who hails from Portsmouth and had previously spent eleven years at the Theatre Royal in Plymouth, has certainly lifted spirits and turned things around. She certainly exudes enthusiasm for the role of the theatre in Colchester:

> Having a theatre gives something very special to the town and adds immeasurable value to the work that is done in schools and the local community. We work with a wide range of people of all ages. We have dance classes for toddlers, activities for the over 50s and classes for people with physical disabilities. We currently have a group of between thirty to forty actors who work with us on and off. There is enough demand to keep some of them employed all year round, either working in the schools or community or on the stage, but for the most part they like to have the flexibility to go off and do a movie or television.

The Fall and Rise of a Landmark

The Town Hall is without doubt the most striking building in Colchester High Street. It dominates the town centre and is a near perfect example of the revived Renaissance style of the late Victorian period. It was opened by the Earl of Rosebery (a former Prime Minister) on 15 May 1902 and so in recent years has celebrated its centenary. But what were the origins of the building, and why was such a grand structure erected in the first place?

To begin, it is worth noting that the present structure is the third in a line of municipal buildings to have occupied the same small plot of land since Norman times. The earliest of these structures, which was known as the Moot Hall, was built in the twelfth century and, amazingly, lasted until 1843, when it finally fell under the axe of the Victorian town planners. Although to the modern eye the old building would have been considered attractive and rather quaint, to those alive at the time it was seen as being cramped and something of an embarrassment. In fact, just a few years earlier, Cromwell in his *History of Colchester* had described the building as being 'mean and insignificant, and totally unworthy of the ancient borough.' Its replacement was a three-storey structure with a classical façade, and although described at the time as being of an elegant and grand design, it too was to be replaced in a little over fifty years. In fact, as early as the 1870s the building was being decried as being of insufficient size, ill-ventilated and inconvenient and moves were afoot to pull it down and re-build. But the feeling was not general and many were horrified at the thought of losing their old Town Hall and suggested that it would be far wiser to let it remain and to extend the building rather than demolish it. And so began a decade or two of discussions and argument as to which was the best way to proceed.

The final decision to demolish the building came in 1897 following a series of damming reports by five independent architects, all of whom considered that the old building's foundations were unstable, and that the best way forward would be to pull it down and start again. The council agreed and it was decided to obtain competitive designs for a new building from a number of eminent architects. Norman Shaw, one of the greatest architects

The present Town Hall. The Author

The Norman Moot Hall which was demolished in 1843. Author's collection

The Victorian Town Hall of 1844–45. Author's collection

John Belcher, architect of the present Town Hall. Author's collection

John Belcher's winning design. Author's collection

of the time, was asked to adjudicate. From a total of eight entries submitted, Mr Shaw awarded first place to Mr John Belcher of London. Belcher's design was grand, impressive and flamboyant and was to become something of a role model for the building of neo-Baroque town halls during the Edwardian period. It also won acclaim from the architectural critics of the day including *The Builder* magazine: 'Mr Belcher shows a fine stately looking plan which combines dignity with efficiency.'

The architect's original estimate to complete the structure was in the region of £36,000, excluding many of the planned external and internal embellishments. In fact, the final cost of construction, which was awarded to the firm of Kerridge and Shaw of Cambridge, came to about £55,000, of which about £12,000 was raised by local benefactors. From the outset the council had adopted the principle that whilst such parts of the building as are necessary for the administration of the town, and for the use of the inhabitants at large, should be erected at public cost, the embellishment of the building, including pictures, statues and stained glass etc, should be funded privately. The largest single gift in this regard was without doubt that made by the Mayor, James Paxman (1897/98), who generously offered to defray the entire cost of the clock tower, which was estimated at about £3,000.

The demolition of the old Town Hall in 1899. Author's collection

The foundation stone for the new building was laid by HRH the Duke of Cambridge (first cousin of Queen Victoria) on 31 October 1898. The giant stone, weighing two tons, was supplied by L J Watts Ltd of Colchester, and had a small hole (12 inches × 9 inches) cut into the top into which was placed a parchment record signed by the mayor, the Duke of Cambridge, and the town clerk, as well as a copy of the official programme of the day's proceedings. The type of stone used is known as Brown Portland, being similar to that

Laying the foundation stone for the new Town Hall in October 1898. Author's collection

Fixing the statue of 'St Helena' to the top of the tower. Pictured clockwise from bottom left are – Gurney Benham, the architect's representative, James Paxman, Wilson Marriage and the Mayor, Claude Egerton Green. Author's collection

A close up view of the statue of 'St Heléna' and one of the ravens on top of the Town Hall. EADT

used for the construction of St Paul's Cathedral. One important announcement made at the time was to the effect that Her Majesty the Queen had given her permission for the tower of the building to be named the 'Victoria Tower' following a request made by James Paxman.

Building work began on 2 January 1899 and was to take just over three years to complete. It had been decided to place a statue of St Helena, the town's patron saint, on top of the tower and the job of securing such a monument was given to Councillor Arthur Jarmin. In pursuit of this quest he apparently travelled as far afield as Italy, but being unable to find a statue of St Helena, and perhaps feeling a little desperate, he finally settled for a statue of the Virgin Mary which he duly had shipped back home. The adapted statue was placed on top of the tower from where it still surveys the surrounding countryside, whilst gazing in the direction of Jerusalem.

Below the statue, and set at the four corners of the tower, were placed four large bronze ravens, which are symbolic of the Port of Colchester. Some readers may recall that just a few years ago one of these ravens fell off the building and landed in the High Street early one morning, narrowly missing a man who was passing on his way to work (what an original excuse for being late for work that would have been!). In order to repair the damaged bird, one of the other ravens had to be temporarily removed to act as a pattern, leaving just two ravens on top of the tower for a prolonged period during 1994.

The new Town Hall was finally opened on 15 May 1902 and, as previously mentioned, the guest of honour was the Earl of Rosebery. There were heavy showers in the morning which resulted in some thinning of the crowds that were expected to witness the occasion, but the event was a success as both the Mayor, Alderman Wilson Marriage, and the Earl of Rosebery gave speeches to the enjoyment of those in attendance.

It is unlikely that anybody alive today will be able to remember the occasion, but the experience of one young Colchester school girl, recorded a few years ago, is perhaps worth mentioning. The girl was Olive Manning (née Bennell) who was born in 1889. During a recorded interview when she was a hundred years old, she spoke fondly of her memories of the period:

> I watched the Town Hall being built. I knew the previous Town Hall and the fire station which was next door in Stockwell Street. I was about twelve when the Town Hall was opened by the Earl of Rosebery. I remember going to walk in and a man saying to me, 'You can't come in here, we don't allow children to come in.' But when I said that my father was on duty there, and gave him his name, he let me pass. And so in I went and he took me all over the building, right to the top, and he put me in a cell and locked me in – because they built the police station underneath.

Today, the Town Hall remains very much a working building at the centre of local life and civic affairs. The building houses the mayor's office, council chamber and

The council chamber during a meeting in December 1996, with the mayor, Councillor Westley Sandford, presiding.
Colchester Borough Council

magistrates' courts, not to mention the great Moot Hall where grand civic events such as the annual oyster feast are held. It is also possible, via appointment, to have a guided tour of the building led by a Blue Badge guide.

Still Going Ape over the Zoo

In the spring of 2003, Colchester Zoo was celebrating two anniversaries – the first being forty years since it opened, and the second being twenty years since the current proprietors, Dominque and Angela Tropeano, became the new owners. Yes it is hard to believe that more than forty years has passed since Colchester Zoo first opened to the public back on Whit Sunday in 1963. Since that time the zoo has grown to become one of the finest zoological parks in Europe, and is regarded as one of East Anglia's major tourist attractions. In fact, the zoo, which is home to more than 1,500 animals and which attracts nearly half a million visitors a year, was voted Large Visitor Attraction of the Year in 2003. So how did this amazing success story begin and what are some of the events and initiatives that has led to its current popularity?

Family favourite – baby Tumba, born 5 December 2004. Colchester Zoo

The original idea of creating a zoological park at Stanway Hall near Colchester was the brainchild of Frank and Helena Farrar who since the early 1950s had been owners of a small zoo in Southport. They had apparently been on the lookout for a suitable site by which to expand their operations in Lancashire for a number of years before happening upon Stanway Hall with its twenty-five acres of adjoining land. The Farrars were immediately impressed and set about securing the necessary planning permission to change the use of the land into a zoological park.

Once the deal had been signed and sealed, orders were despatched to various countries for animals to help stock the zoo. East Africa was the target for cheetahs, crowned cranes, ostriches, jumping hares, monkeys and chimpanzees, while California was chosen to secure some sea-lions and India for bear cubs. Already in stock in Southport, and waiting to be transferred to Colchester, were some multi-coloured ponies, kangaroos, llamas, macaws and a pair of hand-reared lions, the male of which (Rajah) had appeared in a number of major films, including three Tarzan adventures.

Subu, the zoo's male Lion. The Author

The zoo was an instant success with about 14,000 people in attendance over the opening bank holiday weekend. In fact, such was the interest locally from those wanting to attend that large numbers of people, many pushing prams, were forced to walk to the zoo along the road from Colchester as there was insufficient public transport available. It seemed as though half of Colchester was pouring in. Admission fees were initially set at 3/- (15p) for adults and 1/6d (7½ p) for children, which compares with today's £12.99 and £6.99 respectively.

By the end of the first year's trading visitor numbers had risen to nearly 150,000 and the scene was set for steady expansion

A sealion watching visitors in the under-water tunnel! Colchester Zoo

and improvement to the site's infrastructure and facilities. In the late 1960s a section of the lake was fenced off for a flock of pink flamingos and a new 200 foot long monkey house was built. The zoo had also by this time acquired some elephants and in 1972 some rare white rhinos from Natal in South Africa (one of which still survives).

An amusing incident occurred in May 1978 when a huge American bison (Buffalo Bill) escaped from his compound. After spending the night in the surrounding fields, he proceeded to make his way towards the Prettygate area of Colchester where he ended up in a resident's back garden. After being sedated with tranquilliser darts Bill was finally recaptured and taken back to the zoo, but not before becoming something of a local celebrity.

It was about this time that Frank and Helena Farrar began to think seriously about their retirement and a search was begun for a successor to take their place. The zoo was finally sold to the present owners, Dominique and Angela Tropeano, in 1983. Plans were immediately put in place to begin what was to become a long process of upgrading and improvement of the zoo's infrastructure. This was to include the provision of larger cages and enclosures for the animals, as well as suitable viewing areas and access for the public, a process which is only now being finally realised. The Tropeanos have also made the conservation of wild life and the breeding of endangered species among their primary aims, while at the same time maintaining the zoo's popularity with the general public.

Zebras, rhinos and rare zeedonk (a cross between a zebra and a donkey) in the foreground. The Author

Elephants roaming in the Africa Zone, 2005. The Author

One of the most exciting projects which has come to fruition in recent years has been the creation of the Africa Zone. This consists of a number of large enclosures housing such species as elephants, cheetahs, giraffes, ostriches, rhinos and zebras, many of which can be seen mixing together just as they would normally do in their natural habitat. Of particular interest within the large elephant enclosure is three-year-old Kito (b. 6/12/02), the first baby elephant ever to be born at the zoo, and the more recent Jambo (b. 15/3/04). Both of the young male elephants, who weighed in at around fourteen stone each when born, share their home with the zoo's five other elephants – four females and a male. Each of the adult elephants will daily consume the equivalent of up to six bales of hay and drink up to thirty-five gallons (160 litres) of water. These animals also require strict supervision – especially the bull Tembo – who according to Anthony Tropeano (son of the owners) is potentially the most dangerous animal in the park.

The zoo currently employs about 220 full time staff, about a third of whom are directly involved in helping to care for the animals. All of the zoo's keepers undergo an intensive five-stage training programme which allows each keeper to learn about the care and management of a variety of species, before going on to specialise in one particular category or field.

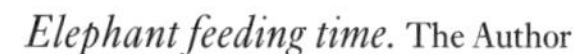

Elephant feeding time. The Author

A colony of leaf-cutter ants attract the attention of these young visitors. Insert: close-up of a leaf-cutter ant at work. The Author

Two of the Zoo's new Siberian tigers, 2005. The Author

Obviously maintaining such a large enterprise is not cheap. At the present time (2005) the daily cost of running the zoo amounts to some £16,000 and this takes no account of any future investment or other capital expenditure. So ticket receipts at the gate are essential to the current and future success of the zoo. In fact, this is the only means by which the future of the zoo will be assured and that new and exciting ways of displaying the large collection of animals to its best advantage will be achieved.

Feeding the giraffes. The Author

Recent initiatives at the zoo include a new £1.75m sea-lion enclosure (opened summer 2003) which includes a twenty-four metre long under-water viewing tunnel. This tunnel is the largest of its kind in any European zoo and attracts large numbers of visitors. The zoo has also been celebrating the recent arrival (July 2005) of three one-year-old captive-bred Siberian tigers (Uri, Anoushka and Czar) from Linton Zoo in Cambridgeshire. The Siberian tiger is a highly endangered species with only about 250 individuals left in the wild, and the current project will form part of a special European breeding programme for these rare animals.

It's Time to go Dutch

As Britain's oldest recorded town and modern day cultural capital of Essex, it is easy to see why Colchester is high on the list of many people's places to visit. The magnificent Norman Castle itself attracts over a 100,000 visitors annually and the adjoining beautifully land-scaped Castle Park provides a refreshing retreat from the hustle and bustle of the modern town. But there is another, oftentimes overlooked, jewel in the town's historic landscape, and one that includes features from just about every period of the town's long history. This is the town's historic Dutch Quarter which is located on a steeply sloping site to the north of the High Street.

The area itself gained its name from the large number of Flemish refugees who settled here during the reign of Elizabeth I to escape religious persecution in their own countries. And the fact that many of these refugees were expert cloth workers, particularly in the manufacture of the new draperies (bays and says), did much to ensure that they received a relatively warm welcome from the town's officials, who were becoming increasingly concerned about the state of their own cloth industry. Within a few years, however, and based almost entirely on the enterprise of these Flemish immigrants, the town had risen from the middling ranks of the cloth manufacturing districts to become one of the top ten cloth making towns in the country – but that is another story.

Let us now then take a brief look at some of the places of interest which are still to be seen in this quiet quarter of the town. One of the oldest buildings still standing in the area is St Helen's Chapel, at the junction of Maidenburgh Street and St Helens Lane. The building was first recorded in 1097, but according to local legend was founded by the Empress Helena herself (the town's patron saint) in the third century. The legend also states that Helena was the daughter of the legendary King Coel of nursery rhyme fame, and that her son, Constantine the Great, was born in Colchester. Of course, this is not entirely true, but whatever the truth of the matter the building certainly stands on foundations dating from the Roman period.

Like most large Roman towns Colchester had a theatre, in fact it had two, and one of those stood right here on the site of St Helen's Chapel. It was built in true Roman style and would have been capable of seating about 3,500 people (compare this with our modern Mercury Theatre, which has a seating capacity of just under 500). If you look carefully at the bricks lining the surface of the street leading up towards the High Street, you will see that they are of alternating colours – red and black – with the black bricks laid

St Helen's Chapel in Maidenburgh Street which stands on the foundations of a Roman theatre. The Author

The author, Patrick Denney, at the site of the foundations of the Roman theatre in Maidenburgh Street. EADT

The house in West Stockwell Street where the author of the rhyme Twinkle Twinkle, Little Star *once lived.* The Author

directly over the surviving foundations of the Roman theatre, which survives just a foot or so below the modern street level. If you were to follow this line of black bricks up the hill you would see where the curve of the former auditorium passes through the row of buildings on the right. Inside the building can be seen the exposed theatre foundations and on one of the walls is a large mural showing how the theatre would have appeared.

You may have noted that we made mention of a famous nursery rhyme in connection with St Helena, but this is not the only nursery rhyme associated with the Dutch Quarter. A short distance away in West Stockwell Street, stands a house (currently Nos. 11 and 12) which was the former home of Isaac Taylor and his family. Isaac's two eldest daughters, Ann and Jane, became famous for writing children's verse and rhyme. Their books went on to become Victorian best sellers and were published worldwide. Perhaps the most famous of their verses, however, and one that was written by Jane in 1806, was something called *Twinkle Twinkle Little Star*.

Just a short distance up the hill from the former Taylor family home is St Martin's Church which dates, in part, from the Norman period, although most of the fabric is medieval. Architecturally, the building looks a little odd because the tower of the church stands no higher than the nave, a result of damage caused by cannon fire during the Siege of Colchester in 1648. Large numbers of Roman bricks can also be seen in the fabric of the building – a common ploy used by medieval builders in a county almost devoid of any natural stone. Although the church closed for religious services in the 1950s, and later became the venue for a local theatre group, the building today is in the care of the Churches Conservation Trust which over the last few years has invested more the £200,000 in its restoration.

Of particular interest in the churchyard is the gravestone of one of the town's former Flemish baymakers who died in the year 1680. His name was Jacob Ringer and we know that he was living in the town during the three-month long Siege of 1648, and was later made to contribute £10 (about £800 in today's money based on the retail price index) towards the hefty fine of £12,000 levied on the town by Thomas Fairfax, the Yorkshire-born Parliamentary general.

St Martin's Church which has lost its tower. The Author

An interior view of St Martin's Church. The Author

Detail of tracery in the chancel window showing the Tetragrammaton (God's name in Hebrew which is usually articulated as Jehovah). The Author

Continuing up West Stockwell Street, one arrives at a curious little graveyard located on the corner of St Runwald's Street. It is curious because unlike like most graveyards there is not a church in sight. In fact, the graveyard has always been isolated from its church (St Runwald's) which, until 1878, used to stand a short distance away in the middle of the High Street. The dedication to St Runwald is also shrouded in mystery as very little

A timber-framed building dating from the fourteenth century in East Stockwell Street. The Author

is known of the origins of the saint other than an extraordinary legend, which although impossible to believe, is worth relating for its amusement factor. Apparently, Runwald was the son of a pagan Northumberland king who had married the Christian daughter of Penda, king of Mercia. He was born at Sutton (thereafter King's Sutton) near Banbury, sometime during the seventh century AD, and died just three days later. And here is where the fun starts, for according to one account of the story, immediately after being born he is said to have cried out three times, 'I am a Christian!' He then asked to be baptised and accepted Holy Communion. Still not finished, he then preached a sermon on the Holy Trinity and the need for virtuous living, whilst quoting freely from the scriptures and the Athanasian Creed. After this he announced his imminent death and chose his place of burial. The infant's life then came to an end – aged just three days!

This is also a good spot from which to view the remaining buildings in the street, which include the former Jacobean-style public library (currently used as a restaurant for council employees), which opened in 1894, and the impressive tower of the Town Hall. On the opposite side of the street is a fine example of a jettied timber-frame building dating from the late 15th century. Although the building has been much altered over the years, it still gives one an impression of the kind of buildings that would have predominated in the area in times past.

CHAPTER 3

MILITARY AND WAR

A Hard Life for Young Conscripts

When Malcolm Firman boarded the London train at his local station back in September 1954, he had little idea that his journey would eventually take him some 28,000 miles around the world – visiting such places as Singapore and Hong Kong – and all at the Queen's expense. For like tens of thousands of other young men at the time, Malcolm was about to commence a two year stint of compulsory national service and his first port of call was to be Warley Barracks, near Brentwood, where he was to join the Essex Regiment.

The concept of conscription, or compulsory National Service, had of course been well tried during both World Wars, and it was still being used in several other countries as a means of bolstering their regular armed forces. In 1948, just three years after the end of the Second World War, the Government decided that conscription into the armed forces should be reintroduced as a permanent feature of the country's defence. The official reason being that if a nation was to survive in the increasingly unsettled state of the world, then it would have to be in a state of readiness and able to defend itself against attack. And so between 1948 and 1960 some two million young men between the ages of eighteen and twenty-six were forced to put their lives on hold as they were drafted into one of the armed forces for a period of two years.

The whole event must have proved a logistical nightmare as thousands of raw recruits were quickly processed and inducted into the military way of life. The first step of the programme consisted of a short period of basic training which everyone had to go through. This was the 'short sharp shock' approach designed to instill a sense of discipline and fitness into the recruits and prepare them for what was to lay ahead; and it was into this environment that Malcolm Firman found himself when he arrived at Warley:

> When we arrived at the station we were bundled into these lorries and taken up the hill to the barracks. Then we were kitted out in army uniform and put into a barrack block. There were boys there from all walks of life, some of whom would probably have been pleased to have owned a good pair of boots for the first time in their lives, while others were people from the landed gentry as it were. On the first day we were told to go down the barbers for a haircut, whether you wanted

> one or not. Some of them were absolutely devastated – many coming from London and being boys that were 'with it'. They lost their hair and, to top it all, you had to pay a shilling for the haircut.

This of course was just the first step in the process of becoming a soldier and over the next few weeks, Malcolm and others like him would experience a form of discipline never before encountered. This largely took the form of a ritual cleaning of just about everything within sight including their boots, the barrack room and sometimes even more challenging things as Malcolm recalls:

> As far as I can remember, I managed with the discipline. There were people there however, and I think that's the reason why I never signed on as a regular, who had got a couple of stripes and they did their best to make everybody's life a misery – there's no other word for it. We had to do barrack room cleaning and things like that, where everything had to be absolutely polished spotless. I mean we even had to go round and whitewash the coal. You'd have a heap of coal and round the outside would be these big lumps of coal which all had to be whitewashed. It was all part of the training: 'If we say you do that, you do that, you

Malcolm Firman looks through some of his many photos from his National Service days. EADT

Malcolm Firman pictured in 1955 whilst serving in Hong Kong and the New Territories. Note the dust on his beret (near the badge) for which he was confined to his barracks for five days. Malcolm Firman collection

Malcolm Firman (second from right) with some old army friends. Second from the left is Den Shipp who was best man at his wedding. Malcolm Firman collection

> don't argue or say, that sounds a bit daft, you do it.' And if you were determined not to do as you were told, you would be put inside. I don't think they would put up with it today.

Malcolm's experience of this seemingly harsh way of life is echoed by many other ex-national servicemen. John Norman, a former Colchester Grammar School boy, and now living at Mistley, was called up in 1948:

> I certainly wasn't looking forward to it, but it was just something we had to do and accept as part of life. When I arrived at the camp I was shuffled into a barrack room and moaned at because I was late. There were about twenty others in the room as well as a sergeant, a corporal and lance corporal who trained you in basic army matters. You'd got to learn to march, to use a rifle, to do PT – you know on the mats and that sort of thing to get you fit. The discipline was very strict, particularly in the first month, because they really tried to make you into a soldier. In other words, to react to any order whether you objected to it or not.

John Norman aged eighteen shortly before he was called up for National Service. John Norman collection

> For example, you might be out on the square drilling and at the end of the session you'd have two minutes to get into your PT kit; and if you didn't get in quick, you were chased or you might get extra boots to shine or something like that. It was chasing you about from morning till night, there was no rest or peace. The idea, of course, was that if someone gave you an order, you'd got to do it and not argue about it because your life, or someone else's life might depend on it.

After the initial period of basic training, the recruits would be assigned to various units for further specialised training before receiving their final posting. Information

John Norman with his old Soldier's Release Book. EADT

regarding these moves and, in fact, almost every other aspect of army life whether it was being told to report for guard duty or perhaps being sent home on leave, was regularly posted on what were called 'Company Orders'. This was in effect a notice board which everybody was required to read and respond to on a regular basis. Malcolm Firman recalls that this was the method by which he received notice of his final posting:

> After training I had three weeks embarkation leave and then I was posted overseas. Each man was given a draft number and your instructions would be posted on 'Company Orders' – a board on which information is posted. It was your responsibility to check these orders on a regular basis. In my case, I was to join the main battalion which was out in Hong Kong. If you neglected to read the orders and consequently failed to turn up for something, you would be put on a charge. It was your responsibility to know what you should be doing at any given time.

As it turned out, both Malcolm Firman and John Norman were assigned to the Far East Land Forces where they completed their remaining service. For some recruits, of course, the main focus of their daily lives would have been centred on simply counting off the days on a calendar until they would be allowed home, but for others it would have been the start of an exciting experience, being able to travel the world, meet new friends, take on responsibility

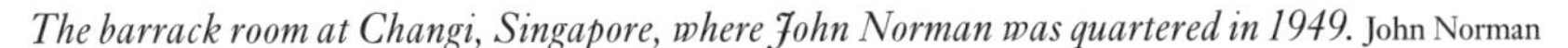

The barrack room at Changi, Singapore, where John Norman was quartered in 1949. John Norman

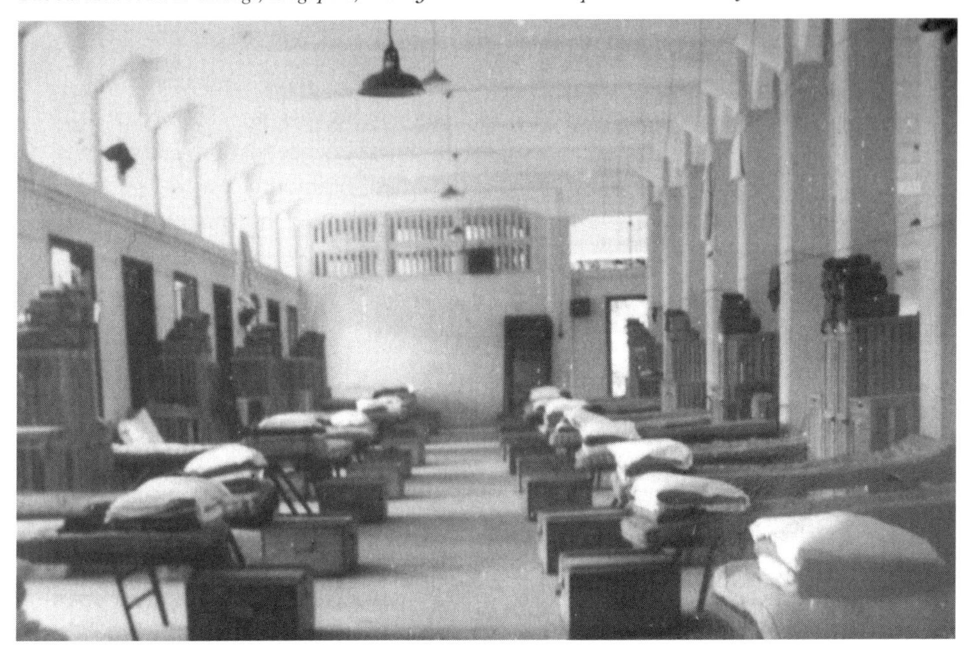

TROOP'S CHRISTMAS DINNER

Tomato Soup

—

Fried Fillet of Cod with Lemon

—

Roast Ribs of Beef au Jus

—

Roast Norfolk Turkey with Stuffing

Garden Peas

Roast and Boiled Potatoes

—

Christmas Pudding, Rum Sauce

—

Fruit Nuts

H.M.T. "ASTURIAS"
At Sea

Saturday, 25th December,
1954

The 1954 Christmas menu from HM troop ship Austuria. *The meal was eaten by Malcolm Firman and his colleagues in the middle of the Indian Ocean.* Malcolm Firman collection

and generally develop as an individual. But regardless of how you fared, or took to military life, most were nevertheless glad to come home. For John Norman, it couldn't have come sooner:

> When I finally got home, it was a great relief. I didn't really enjoy the experience like some people did. Back home, my father had died just before I was called up and my mother and sister were having a hard time of things. At the end of the day, it is difficult to assess the value of the experience. You certainly came home more worldly than those who hadn't been in those circumstances, because at that time the Far East and places like that weren't the sort of places that many people went.

Malcolm Firman, on the other hand, was perhaps a little more positive about the experience:

> I wouldn't have missed doing National Service for the world. It was an experience that I would never have had in any other way. I got to travel and went to places that I would never have seen.

A Perilous Life on the Ocean Waves

When seventeen-year-old Frank Brinkworth joined the Merchant Navy as a bell boy in 1937, he had little idea that within three years he would be caught up in the thick of war, ferrying troops and ammunition to the war front, and witnessing destruction and loss of life on a scale he could never have imagined. This, of course, was the lot of all merchant seamen at the time whose ships and crews were commandeered to help with the war effort, and everyone was expected to do their bit to help. However, despite putting their lives on the line almost every day and night as they braved the hostile waters of the North Atlantic and other supply routes, their exploits and general involvement in the war have to some extent been forgotten over the years, a situation which has only recently been put to right.

Frank Brinkworth, aged eighty-one, wearing his campaign medals from the Second World War. EADT

A major step in this direction has been the recent establishment of a nationally recognised Merchant Navy Day, which has helped to focus and bring together the activities of various veteran groups around the country. On a local level, the setting up of the Harwich & District Merchant Navy Association in June 2000 has also been well received, with membership already passing the one hundred mark. The group was set up by just four founder members – Bill Brown, Kate Wilson, Chris Barker and Rodney Gates – and just eighteen people attended the inaugural meeting. Since then, however, the average meeting attendance has risen dramatically. The group provides a forum for both serving and retired merchant seaman to meet together for social activities and other planned events. Although centred in Harwich, a town with strong naval links, the group welcomes members from all over the district and even has one member who lives as far away as Liverpool and two more from Wales.

As might be expected, the monthly meetings are largely taken up with socialising, which allows plenty of time for reminiscing, particularly about memories of the war years with everyone having equally interesting stories to tell. Frank Brinkworth is typical of the membership and was happy to recall some of his exploits. He remembered when the war began and being 'asked' if he would like to join the Navy:

> The war broke out just as we were approaching Cape Town. When we docked, the ship was stripped of all passengers and sent somewhere else, and we were asked if we would like to join the navy. They wanted us to crew an armed merchant cruiser because they couldn't get the reserves out in time. I was only twenty at the time and we spent the next year patrolling the South Atlantic – God knows what would have happened if we'd have met anything because we were only amateurs really. Anyway, we were provided with naval uniforms and I was trained as a gunner to fire the ship's six inch guns.

After about a year Frank was sent back to England where he rejoined the merchant fleet as an able seaman. He then did a spell sailing with the Atlantic convoys and recalled seeing a large tanker break completely in two during a period of particularly rough weather, recalling that the other ships could only look on as the vessel floundered, unable to assist due to the extreme conditions. One of Frank's most terrifying moments occurred in April 1943 when he was assigned to a ship called the *Fort Ann,* which was bound for North Africa loaded with tanks, shells and other equipment for the landing force. Frank recalls that most of the trip went smoothly until the day before they were due to arrive in Algiers, and then all hell broke loose:

> I was on the wheel at the time and we were all cruising along nicely, you know, keeping in line with the convoy, when all of a sudden the ship in front was hit by a torpedo, and before I could recover, we got it. The first thing that I remember was seeing this Sherman tank, which had been lashed down onto the hatch in front of the bridge, go up past the window in front of me and then fall down

Frank Brinkworth (left) with fellow seaman Arthur Lavarus in 1940. Frank Brinkworth collection

again. Of course, we all quickly abandoned ship and were picked up by an American torpedo boat which then kept going round and round dropping depth charges all over the place. I suppose he must have known what he was doing, but to us it seemed like they were in a blind panic. We were later transferred to a destroyer and given blankets and something to eat and drink. However, just as we were about to settle down for the night an order went out, 'Stand by to Ram.' This, of course, meant full speed ahead and that we were going to hit something. I remember us all grabbing hold onto whatever we could and hearing the engines throbbing away and the guns firing. The target turned out to be a free French submarine which hadn't given a recognition signal quickly enough. The next morning we heard news that our ship was still afloat and we were asked if we would be willing to re-board her and take her on into Algiers, which of course we did at a very slow pace, even though we weren't too happy about going back onto an ammunition ship.

Frank Brinkworth pictured on board his first ship, the Garth Castle, *where he was employed as a bell boy.* Frank Brinkworth collection

Whilst Frank's memories are typical of many of the group's war-time experiences, other members who served in slightly more recent times have equally interesting stories to tell. One such person is Kate Wilson who is the only female member of the group. In fact, Kate's claim to fame is that she was part of the first ever all-female stewarding crew on a merchant cargo ship. The year was 1947 and seventeen-year-old Kate had applied for a job as a cabin girl on the *La Cordillera*, a purpose-built ship which was going to have an all female catering crew as part of a new experimental venture in British shipping. Kate recalls receiving a telegram asking her to report immediately to Liverpool, where she was to join the ship:

> I got to Liverpool and was issued with my uniform before joining the rest of the crew. The blokes on the ship thought it was wonderful, but a lot of the seamen didn't want us in Liverpool because they thought we were taking their jobs and we did get a bit of barracking. We did the same jobs as the men and got paid the same as them. I started off as a cabin girl and was assigned to the midships

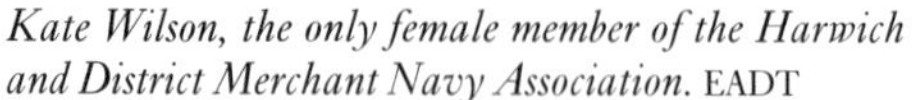

Kate Wilson, the only female member of the Harwich and District Merchant Navy Association. EADT

Kate Wilson, aged seventeen, aboard the La Cordillera *in 1947.* Kate Wilson collection

> pantry, where I looked after the engineering and deck officers. We cleaned their cabins and served their food from the galley. We worked from 6.30 in the morning to whatever time we finished at night, seven days a week. There was no particular training given, we just picked up the job as we went along. But being mainly domestic work it was something that most girls at the time were already used to.

Like most people going to sea for the first time, Kate suffered from initial bouts of sea sickness, a problem which she hadn't given a second thought to in her overwhelming desire to go to sea:

> At first I suffered badly from sea sickness and I would have walked off the ship if I had been able to do so. We left Liverpool on the afternoon tide and I had never considered being seasick. I was so desperate to go I would have put up with anything. I was ill for about four weeks but then things gradually got better. I remember that we were feted by the press wherever we went and interviewed for radio and the newspapers, who were all rather intrigued by this novel all-women crew. We had a whale of a time. It was really exciting.

Beyond the Call of Duty

During the first week of June 2004, some 25,000 Britons made the journey to Normandy to commemorate the 60th anniversary of the D-Day landings. Among them were hundreds, if not thousands, of veterans who each had their own special memories of that colossal operation in which over 150,000 men were shipped across the channel in a flotilla of boats to be landed on the beaches of Normandy. Here follows the experiences of four local men who took part in that momentous exercise and lived to tell the tale.

George Young

One of the veterans who made the journey to Normandy was Major George Young who was in charge of B Company, 6th Battalion, Green Howards when they landed on Gold Beach at H+20 (07.45) on 6 June 1944. He recalled that earlier reconnoitring of the beach area by submarine had shown that there was a short stretch of sand to be crossed, followed by a minefield surrounded by barbed wire, and then an anti-tank ditch. The plan therefore was to make their way as quickly as possible across the beach without stopping and to get beneath the wire surrounding the minefield as it was thought extremely unlikely that the Germans would have had any lines of fire trained on that particular area. For according

Major George Young wearing his medals including the Military Cross. The Author

Major George Young during his army days. George Young collection

to George, 'Even the Germans wouldn't have thought that anyone was foolish enough to crawl under the wire into a mine field!' However, even the best-laid schemes do not always go according to plan and, as George recalls, it all very nearly went horribly wrong:

> As we approached the beach we went down the scrambling nets off the side of the mother ship and got into the landing craft. Finally we reached the shore. The naval officer commanding the landing craft ordered the front to go down and then he saluted me and said, 'There you are Sir', and I said, 'Thank you' and then stepped off into at least seven feet of water and the boat went over the top of me. I can clearly remember kicking out with my left foot and finally hitting this big bolt which was sticking out underneath and being shot out to the side [and away from the propellers!] and I struggled to the shore. In the meantime, of course, the boat had gone forward and everyone had got off. Anyway, there I am struggling up the beach shouting 'I'm in charge' and the men were already underneath the wire waiting for the tanks to arrive. These were the flail tanks which were going to flail us through the minefield.
>
> The tanks finally got us through the minefield and we all lined up in the anti-tank ditch ready to attack the ridge which was in front of us. The ditch had very steep sides and although myself and the Sergeant Major got up okay, it wasn't long before we realised that we were walking along by ourselves – the men were each carrying so much equipment that as much as they tried to climb out of the ditch they kept falling down again. Anyway, we decided that we would walk on and see if anybody was going to fire at us, because I was sure that in a moment or two they were going to start. But nobody fired and we walked on, and by this time of course the men were beginning to get out of the ditch, and on we went, and then we saw them [the Germans], and they were in a trench just looking at us. They made no attempt to fire at us, no attempt to show their weapons or anything – they just sat in the trenches looking at us. I remember opening up a packet of cigarettes which still had the cellophane on and which, of course, hadn't got wet with my little dive and throwing some towards them whilst shouting out 'Zurück' (get behind me). We took about 120 prisoners.

George and his company pressed on for several kilometres until they arrived at a small village called Crepon where they were joined by the rest of the battalion. By D-Day plus four, they had progressed to a position near the village of Creully and it was from near there that they were ordered into an attack which proved to be disastrous:

> It was a terrible battle. We were still trying to contact the Germans and we had a suspicion they were lying in wait for us in a nearby wood. Anyway, a tank was sent up ahead to see if the coast was clear and we heard back that there was nobody in the wood. As it turned out, the Germans had let the tank come up and then go away again. What we should have done, of course, was to have left

> the first tank there and then sent up another one. However, the Brigadier gave the order to advance and just as we got half way across this meadow towards the wood all hell was let loose. We suffered terrible losses, and that was when I was wounded. One of soldiers not far from me got hit and I crawled over to him – there were shells dropping and machine gun bullets flying all over the place – and I got hold of him and brought him back into company head-quarters. As I stood up to get my first field dressing out a shell went off behind me and some shrapnel went through my arm and into my back. After lying there for some while I was picked up by one of the tanks which was going back. They managed to hold me on the front of the tank, and with all these bullets flying all over the place, got me back to the dressing station.
>
> And that was the beginning of the end for me as far as the war was concerned. I was later awarded the Military Cross for helping this wounded soldier and for various other actions performed on that day, but I never saw any action again.

At the time of the anniversary, George was the highest ranking surviving officer from the 6th Battalion, Green Howards which took part in the D-Day landings and, as such, was invited to attend a ceremony held at Crepon where he accepted the salute from surviving members of his Battalion.

Os Avis

Os Avis served as a bombardier in the 147th Regiment of the Essex Yeomanry and may be the only surviving former member of the Essex Yeomanry still living in Colchester who actually landed on D-Day. Before the war Os worked for the Colchester Electricity Board and can recall the occasion when he and several of his work colleagues were invited to join the Colchester Territorials who were in the process of forming another regiment:

Normandy veteran, Oz Avis from Colchester. The Author

> I can remember Major Turner coming round and saying that they are forming a new regiment and that they were looking for volunteers. A meeting was held in the Town Hall and virtually every-one who worked in the various council departments turned up. Many of us decided to join and we ended up spending a couple of evenings a week practising in

Oz Avis (second from right) with other members of the Essex Yeomanry. Oz Avis collection

the old Drill Hall in Stanwell Street. When war was declared we were all called up and had to report to our temporary barracks down on Hythe Quay.

In the months leading up to the D-Day landings we became attached to the 8th Armoured Brigade and spent some time practising our landings up in Scotland. As we moved closer to D-Day we were finally told that we would be going to France, but that was all, we didn't know where. We were also each given 200 French francs and told to write a will in the event that we didn't make it home.

On 1st June we started loading up the LCT (landing craft tank) with a number of bren-gun carriers. We set sail from Southampton on 4 June, but had to turn back because of the bad weather. We had to remain in the boats until the following morning before setting sail again. There were hundreds of boats there – if the German airforce had come over then they would have had a wonderful target, but we never saw them. We travelled all the way over in the landing craft which held about five or six of us as well as the bren-gun carriers. The sea was very rough and this flat-bottomed boat was going up and down, crashing onto the waves, and we were all seasick. After we had sailed about half-way across we were finally told that we were going to Normandy and that we were gong to land on Gold Beach. The guns which we were carrying had to go in first because they had to provide close support for the infantry, and ours were the first ones in from our regiment.

As we neared the Normandy coast there was a terrific barrage going on from our war ships, with all their guns firing. The rocket ships used to go in and turn parallel to the beach before letting off their rockets. I remember thinking to myself that nobody could possibly live through that. When we got near to the shore at about H+60 (08.25) myself and two colleagues, Fred Williams and Joe Waterhouse (who incidentally was very short in stature), were told to put on our oilskins and get ready to jump out and push this huge coconut matting into the water so that our bren-gun carriers could get a better grip on the bottom of the sea. When the front went down we jumped into the water which came up to our chests, although little Joe's head was almost submerged. And, of course, with there still being some air caught in our oilskins we were bobbing about like corks for some time before the air was expelled. Anyway, we started pushing this mat out but little Joe's head was nearly under the water so I had to hold on to one of his hands while Fred held onto the other, and in this way we pushed this thing towards the beach. The sea itself was full of these stakes with mines on the end and some had got broken off during the bombardment and they were coming along and hitting us on the chest, on the head, all over – but thankfully they never went off. Eventually we got this mat out and walked ashore. I was so pleased to get off the boat and to get on land.

We eventually got off the beach and made our way across this field where we stopped alongside this huge hole – big enough to hold two corporation buses – which had been made by the bombs coming over in the night. And as I was standing there looking at this hole, a twig with a handkerchief tied to it suddenly appeared nearby and that was my first encounter with the enemy. Two Germans got out and fortunately I had my sten-gun with me. I can remember chuckling to myself because one of these German soldiers was about 6 ft 6 inches tall and other one only five foot and they reminded me of the famous comic book characters Tired Tom and Weary Willy. They came towards me and I beckoned them to put their hands up and told them to go down to the beach.

Felix Johnson

Felix Johnson was a quartermaster sergeant in the Herts and Essex Yeomanry at the time of the invasion and can remember being sealed up in an Army camp on the outskirts of London as they waited for the order to depart for France:

Towards the end of May 1944 we were sent to a camp near Wanstead Flats to prepare for D-Day. We were encircled by barbed wire with guards posted

Normandy veteran Felix Johnson from Colchester. The Author

Felix Johnson as a young soldier. Felix Johnson collection

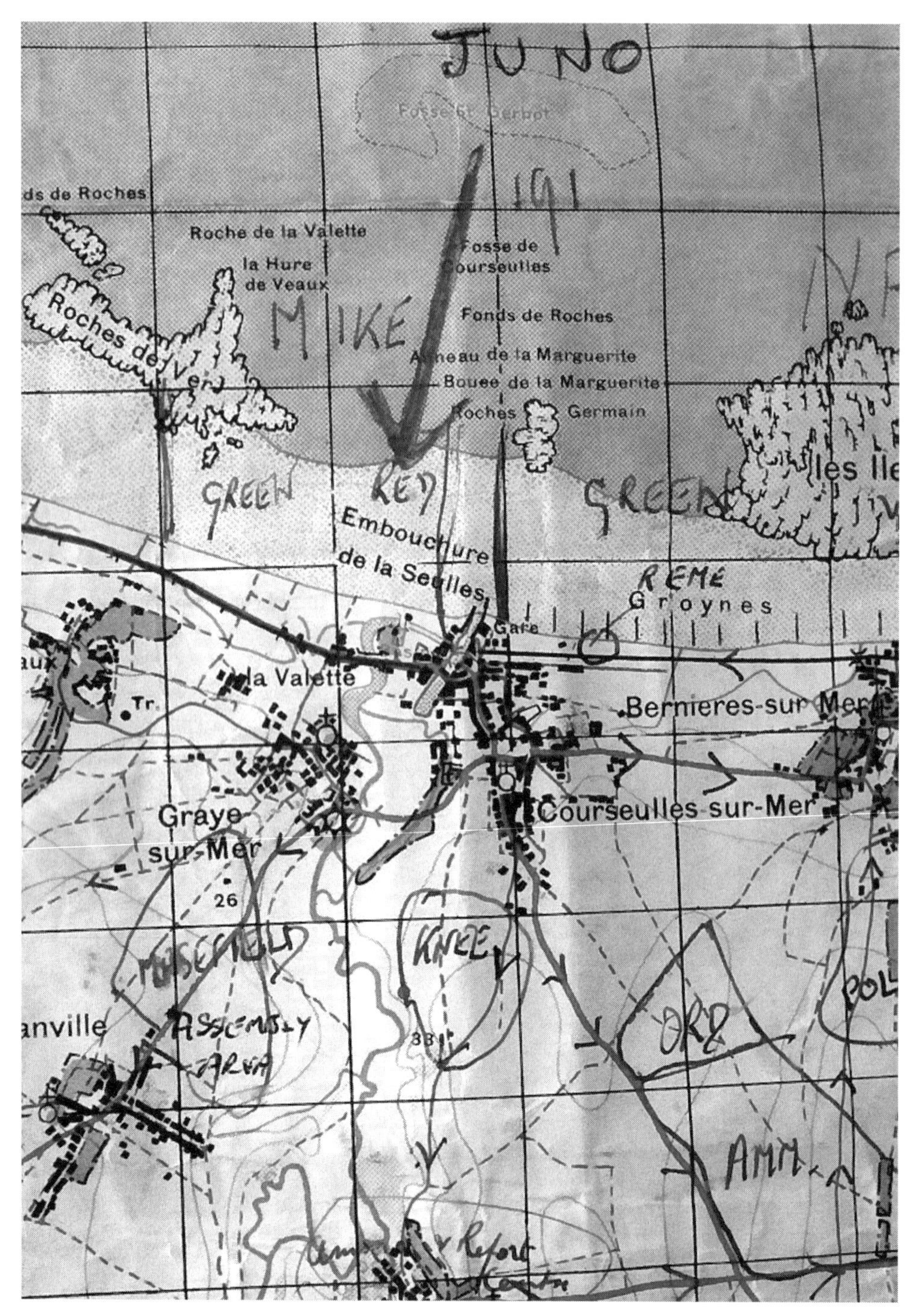

Part of a map issued to Felix Johnson on D-Day. Felix Johnson collection

all round – nobody could get in or out. And it was then that we were told that we were going to France. We waited and waited and then on the morning of 6 June we heard about the invasion on the radio and were immediately put on parade and told that we were going to be loaded onto the ships that same day. By this time I was just wanting to get on with it. We were finally taken down to the docks where we got on to one of these Liberty ships which each held about 300 men. We set sail about 6.30 pm that evening and went down the Thames to a point off Southend pier where we stopped to wait for the whole convoy to get together. We remained there throughout the next day before finally moving off on the morning of 8 June. As luck would have it, just as we were about half way across the Straits of Dover, our ship broke down and we were left stranded as the rest of the convoy sailed on. We were left behind like a sitting duck for any German guns or U-Boats that happened to be around, but I expect that by this time they had more important matters to concern them.

We finally got going again and caught up with the convoy just as it was approaching the coast of Normandy. There were literally hundreds of ships lying off-shore – as far as the eye could see. That night we anchored alongside HMS *Rodney* and I can remember an order going out for everyone to get below deck. At first we wondered what was going on and then we heard the throbbing of the engine of a German bomber. Then all hell was let loose. The battleship opened up with its anti-aircraft guns and shrapnel was raining down on the metal deck like a hailstorm. Then we understood the reason for the order to get below.

The next morning (9 June) after transferring to a landing craft, we headed for Juno beach. We ran in to within about 100 yards from the shore before driving off the ramp into about two feet of water. My orders were to take my truck, which was carrying six men and various essential stores, to an assembly area about one mile from the beach, and then onto the village of Cainet. Throughout this time the battleships and cruisers were still firing over our heads to positions inland. Although we had been in the Army for more than four years we were still very green. We had never seen any action and we had no idea what to expect.

Arthur Parsonson

Arthur Parsonson, a former Mayor and Honorary Alderman of Colchester, was attached to 413 Battery of the Essex Yeomanry which landed on Gold Beach at about 08.15 hours on D-Day. Arthur was on board a landing craft which was carrying several tanks belonging to the Sherwood Rangers Yeomanry as well as a number of soft top vehicles on the upper deck. Having been afloat since about 06.00 on the morning of 4th June – a total

Arthur Parsonson with his soldier's pay book. EADT

of more fifty hours in rough seas – they were relieved to have finally arrived at their destination:

> We were due to arrive off the beach about 11 in the morning but we got there about a quarter past eight. As we ran into the beach they started to lower the ramp but they didn't get it right and instead of it stopping in the horizontal position, it went right down to the bottom. The water was obviously too deep and try as they may they couldn't get it up again. And, of course, with the ramp stuck in the down position we couldn't get into shallower water either. We eventually had to offload the tanks and other vehicles onto these large raft type structures which were called Rhinos. They were about the size of two or three tennis courts and were supported by a number of oil drums to keep them afloat – they also had an engine fitted at each corner. Well we managed to get one of these Rhinos lashed to the front of our landing craft and were then able to unload the tanks. Even so it wasn't an easy operation. I remember telling one of the drivers of the tanks that when he drove off to make sure that he headed straight for the centre of the raft as quickly as possible, and that when he saw the next tank came off to drive as fast as he could to the far corner so that it didn't turn over.
>
> By the time we eventually got ashore several of our tanks had been hit by a German gun emplacement which was causing us a few problems. Fortunately it was knocked out by one of our SPs [self-propelled guns]. The commander of the SP was Sergeant Palmer who had bravely got out of his gun and directed his driver to a position where he could have a good go at the pill box. The first shell that he fired hit the stonework, but the second scored a direct hit, falling right down the slit of the gun opening. Sergeant Palmer was later awarded the Military Cross for that. At one of our previous reunions at Le Hamel, the Essex Yeomanry Association fitted a plaque to the pill box (which is still there) as

Troops from the Essex Yeomanry on the beaches in Normandy. Arthur Parsonson collection

a reminder of Sergeant Palmer's heroic actions, and as a memorial to those members of the Essex Yeomanry who gave their lives for the liberation of Europe.

I was There as Nazis Signed Peace

For one Essex man the end of the war with Germany in May 1945 will be remembered with extreme clarity and detail. Because Tom Wiseman, an eighty-nine-year-old resident of Birch, on the outskirts of Colchester, was actually present in the same building in which the surrender documents were signed. At the time he was working within a small team employed in decoding secret messages which were constantly being relayed to General Eisenhower's headquarters at Rheims in north eastern France, and in the early hours of the morning of 7 May 1945, he stood and watched history being made as the German war machine finally capitulated.

Tom was born at Sible Hedingham in 1916, but shortly afterwards moved to Colne Engaine where he spent the rest of his childhood. He attended nearby Earls Colne Grammar School and later became a student teacher in the village before attending a teacher training college in London. By the outbreak of war in 1939 he had graduated from the training college and had secured his first teaching post at a primary school at Wivenhoe.

Tom Wiseman recalls the signing of the German surrender at Rheims on May 7, 1945, although peace was not celebrated until the following day at the request of the Americans. The Author

Tom Wiseman pictured at Karachi on route to Australia in June 1945. Tom Wiseman collection

However, his new found career was soon to be interrupted following the arrival of his call-up papers in May 1940. Opting successfully to join the Royal Air Force he spent the next three years engaged in a number of fairly routine activities, including a spell working as a wireless operator and also for an extended period working at an air gunnery school in South Wales, helping to prepare targets for trainee air gunners to fire at. However, feeling that his skills could be put to much better use, he was anxious to move on to something else and was finally chosen to train as a code and ciphering officer at Worchester. After successfully completing that course he was despatched to work at the Headquarters of Coastal Command, located in an underground chalk quarry at Chatham.

The turning point in his wartime career, however, came in the early months of 1944 when he was called upon to attend a special interview in London. This was when he first became associated with a team that was involved in deciphering German signals at Bletchley Park. Tom can still recall details of that interview and his induction into the secretive world of code-breakers:

> When I first arrived at this address in London I had no idea what was happening. I was marched into an office by a sergeant, stood there and was told by a senior army officer that I had been selected to do some very important work which would involve the Official Secrets Act. I was then interviewed by this officer who then handed me a copy of the Official Secrets Act and told me to carefully read through the relevant sections. When I looked up, he said, 'Do you

> understand it?' I said, 'Yes Sir', so he told me to read it again to make sure. So I read it again and he said, 'Do you understand it, are you quite, quite sure?' to which I replied in the affirmative. At this stage in the proceedings an air force Squadron Leader suddenly appeared from behind some curtains, put a revolver into my ribs, and said, 'If from this moment on you divulge anything that you learn it will be my duty to shoot you on the spot.' And with that I was inducted into the team and despatched with a number of others to join up with the First United States Army Group (FUSAG) whose headquarters were in Bryanston Square, near Marble Arch.

Shortly after D-Day on 6 June 1944, Tom and his unit were sent across to Normandy to follow on behind the American Army which by now was beginning to move eastwards towards Paris. He can still clearly remember details of the journey across the Channel and the fact that when they arrived in France they received a rather hostile reception from some of the French peasantry:

> We travelled over to Normandy on one of the Liberty ships and because we were carrying such sensitive equipment, all of our trucks had to be stored on the deck alongside the ship's bulwarks, which could easily be lowered in an emergency, and our vehicles rolled over the side should we have come under serious attack from a German naval craft, or indeed have been sunk by enemy aircraft. Better to have our equipment scattered across the sea bed rather than let it fall into enemy hands. Even our code books, and other important papers, had to be kept in special canvas bags designed to flood when in contact with water, so that if the ship was sunk nothing of importance could be salvaged by the enemy. And as far as the rather frosty reception that we received from some of the French locals is concerned, I believe this must have been because they mistook us for German prisoners of war because we were still wearing our 'air force blue' uniforms and, of course, they had got so used to seeing the British and American servicemen in their traditional khaki.
>
> By the end of 1944 we had moved on to Versailles and were quartered not far away from the Palace itself. Our job throughout this period had been to receive messages from Bletchley Park, most of which had originally been intercepted from the Germans via various radio reception stations scattered throughout the countryside. The team at Bletchley then decoded and translated the signals before re-encoding them and then sending them on to Special Liaison Units (SLUs) such as ours. Each SLU team was made up of nine men and we worked in groups of three doing an eight hour shift around the clock. After we had received an encoded message from Bletchley (and they were coming in more or less continually), our task was to unscramble the message, using our special Typex machines (similar to the German Enigma machine) before

> passing the information on to the relevant army officer or department. The machines that we used were quite complicated and had numerous keys and codes which were alternated at random every few hours.

By the spring of 1945 Tom's unit had moved on to General Eisenhower's Supreme Allied Headquarters at Rheims which was located in a newly built French technical school. The school buildings were set around a large quadrangle with access via an arched entranceway. Tom recalls that his team were located in some offices on the first floor of the main building, just two or three doors away from where General Eisenhower and other high ranking officers were stationed. And it was from this building on the evening of 6 May, that Tom first became aware that something out of the ordinary was taking place:

> On that particular evening I happened to be on duty – overnight from eight o'clock until six in the morning. And I can remember looking out of the

Historic moment: the signing of the Surrender at Rheims as depicted by a specially commissioned French artist. 1. Lt General Sir F.E Morgan (British Army); 2. Major General Seveze (witness for the French); 3. Admiral Burroughs, Chief of Staff, British Navy; 4. Lt General Bedell Smith, US Army; 5. Col Zenkovitch (Russian interpreter); 6. General Souslaporov, Chief of Soviet Mission; 7. General Spaatz, US Air Force; 8. Admiral von Friedenburg, Commander in Chief, German Navy; 9. General Jodl, Chief of Staff to Admiral Doenitz, German High Command; 10. Col Oxenius, Chief of Staff, Luftwaffe. Tom Wiseman collection

The Allied headquarters building at Rheims where the Surrender was signed. Tom Wiseman

> window and realising that there was a great deal of movement going on. The guard of American soldiers seemed to have been reinforced very strongly and, at about midnight, a convoy of very important looking vehicles started making its way through the arched entranceway, which was more or less just below our office window. I realised that these were VIPs of one sort or another and they were immediately ushered into the building and taken into one of the rooms used by the more senior officers which was located just up the corridor from where I was on duty. And although I was not fully aware of what was happening at the time, I had a pretty good idea of what was taking place. And at precisely 2.41 am on the morning of 7 May, General Jodl, Chief of Staff of the German Army, signed the Instrument of Surrender on behalf of the German High Command, thereby bringing to an end the war in Europe.

In fact, General Jodl signed three other surrender documents at the same time – one each for Great Britain, Russia and France. The signing took place in the presence of a number of allied officers including, Lt. General Bedell Smith (representing General Eisenhower who had apparently refused to meet with the Germans until after the surrender had been signed), General Sousloparov (on behalf of the Soviet High Command), and Major General Sevez (who was present as a witness for France).

The Russians, however, who believed that the continued fighting in the east between Germany and the Soviet Union made the Rheims surrender look like a separate peace, made a request to Supreme Headquarters Allied Expeditionary Forces (SHAEF) that the surrender ceremony be repeated in Berlin the following day. This was agreed and despite requests from Winston Churchill and King George VI that the victory should be celebrated on Monday, 7 May, they finally bowed to American wishes that this be delayed to 8 May. And, of course, when the official announcement finally came declaring that the war in Europe was finally over it sparked off a wave of celebrations and street parties.

In Rheims Tom Wiseman found himself partying along with the rest of the community late into the night:

> There was lots of dancing and singing in the streets of Rheims and a large bonfire was lit in the main boulevard. Of course, we joined in with the celebrations; and being just a small number of Royal Air Force personnel, the French people were very happy to see us, and we were well looked after. It was a glorious occasion and the war in Europe, at least, was over. A few days later, however, we were flown back to the UK by Dakota and I was given embarkation leave to be with my wife Joan whom I had met and married earlier in the war.

Back home in England Joan Wiseman had also become caught up in the celebrations. She had spent the war years serving in the WAAF and remembers being stationed in London at the time of the surrender:

> I can remember doing the conga down Regent Street and Oxford Street. There were hundreds of us, army, navy, air force, everyone. Buses were hooting and all sorts of things. We all ended up outside Buckingham Palace where we saw the King and Queen and the Princesses on the balcony. There were thousands of people there with everyone shouting, screaming and singing their heads off. And, of course, the blackout had been lifted and the celebrations went on late into the night. It was the end of six years of war and everyone just went mad. It was a feeling of great relief.

Joan Wiseman, aged twenty-five, pictured in her WAAF uniform in 1941. Tom Wiseman collection

While the rest of the nation was busy celebrating the 60th anniversary of VE Day on 8 May 1945, Tom and Joan Wiseman were also looking forward to another celebration just a few weeks later when they were due to celebrate sixty-one years of married life together. And, of course, back in 1945, although the war in Europe had come to an end, the war in the Far East was still raging on and would continue to do so for a further three months. So after enjoying a short spell of leave back in England, Tom was soon on board a plane heading for Australia where his team continued working for the Australian Army and Air Force until the surrender of Japan in August later in the year. Remarkably, yet again, Tom was present at that surrender also.

He recalls that they were flown out in stages to Australia, from were they were dispersed in smaller groups to various parts of the western Pacific:

> After spending a few weeks at General Blamey's headquarters in Brisbane, a small group, including myself, were flown to New Guinea, and then on to Morotai. We set up camp in a coconut grove and our work with the Typex machine, via Bletchley Park, continued as before, but by now the work was very routine. And because we had to work fairly short shifts, we didn't see enough of the messages coming through to be able to form a clear picture of what was going on. Although we knew that the Americans were trying to get as near to Japan as they could, we didn't know that the atom bomb on Hiroshima was coming.

The signing of the Japanese Surrender on the Island of Morotai on September 9, 1945. Tom Wiseman

One day I remember we were told to get dressed (because at that time we were more or less living in our shorts), and to make our way out to this large air-landing strip, which had been set up on the east side of the Island. When we arrived we found that hundreds of other people were assembling and we knew that something important was going on. In fact, there was a whisper going round that the Japanese were going to come in and surrender.

So the eight or nine of us RAF chaps made sure that we got near the front row, and managed to get behind the trestle table where the officers of the Australian army were seated. Fortunately, there was a gap through which I could see across the open parade ground and I was able to take some photographs of what was going on. Then, when everyone appeared to be assembled, these Japanese officers were marched up by the military police and ordered to sign the surrender. First they drew their swords and laid them on the table in front of the Australian officers which, of course, was the main action of surrender. And then after laying down their swords they stepped forward to sign on the dotted line.

The surrender which Tom witnessed was, in fact, one of several formal surrender documents signed by the Japanese. The main surrender ceremony, which had taken place

Tom and Joan Wiseman who celebrated their 61st wedding anniversary in June 2005. The Author

on board the USS battleship *Missouri* in Tokyo Bay on 2 September, was followed by other signings in various parts of the Pacific arena. A week later, on Morotai Island, where Tom was based at the headquarters of the Australian Forces, General Thomas Blamey accepted the surrender of Lt-General Teshima, commander of the Japanese Second Army, which comprised 126,000 men. The official record states that on being ordered to sign the document, General Teshima saluted, unbuckled his sword and, after bowing, proffered it as the token of a beaten foe. He then sat down and signed deliberately and unhurriedly, rose again and saluted. Signatures were then added by the Japanese navel officers Captain Totu Oyama and Captain Minoru Toyama. General Blamey then added his own name to the document indicating his acceptance of the surrender. He then made a strong speech directed at the Japanese delegation during which he severely criticised their actions in the theatre of war, and added that he didn't recognise them as an honourable and gallant foe. The event took place in front of an assembly of some 10,000 Australian and allied troops.

As for Tom Wiseman, he was at last able to relax a little whilst waiting for a lift back home. Finally, after waiting several months and spending yet another Christmas away from his family, he boarded the troop ship *Multan* in early January 1946 and spent most of the five week long journey home playing cribbage on the top deck in the hot sun.

Freed From a Jungle Hell

Charles Jones, a Londoner by birth who later settled in the Colchester area and became a well-known local school teacher, was a member of the 'Forgotten Army'. Despite the surrender of the German forces in Europe in May 1945, the war continued to rage in the Far East for several months resulting in further suffering to thousands of Allied prisoners of war. The conditions in which these men were kept was appalling and when their release finally came, following the Japanese surrender in August 1945, the bodies of most had been reduced to little more than skeletons, racked with disease. Charles was one of these men.

Charles Jones, former Far East PoW, pictured in 1997. Mary Jones

He had joined the Territorials at Lea Green in south-east London in April 1939 and was attached to the 65th Field Regiment, 8th London. When war broke out in September 1939 he was called to muster with his regiment at Woolwich Barracks and for the next two years worked as a signaller with 259 Battery in various parts of the United Kingdom. In October 1941, however, his regiment sailed from Liverpool for America where they joined with the rest of the 18th Infantry Division for the long trip to the Far East. They arrived in Bombay in late December before moving on to Singapore which, or course, by this time was being strongly targeted by the Japanese.

In fact, Charles didn't have long to wait for his first encounter with the enemy. For just a few weeks later, and as the Japanese Army was fast advancing towards their position, he was sent out with three colleagues to try and lay a cable to one of their forward gun positions, and was extremely lucky to escape with his life:

> As my mate and I were pulling the cable from the vehicle, a Jap shell hit the truck, killing the two other men who were still on board. We were given another truck and continued on our way to the forward observation post. It was a really terrible place to be. The firing was intense and the Japs were all around us.

But as Charles was to shortly find out this was to be merely a foretaste of the horrors which lay ahead. For just two days later news arrived that the British had surrendered

Charles Jones (front row left) with his comrades in the Far East a few weeks before they were captured. Mary Jones collection

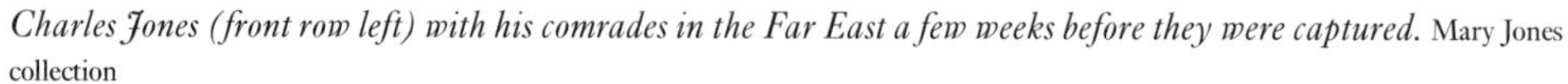

and within twenty-four hours the Japanese had arrived and taken Charles and his comrades prisoner. They were immediately forced to march fifteen miles to Changi Barracks on the north of the island, and anyone who was particularly slow, or broke ranks for any reason along the route was badly beaten – an alarming indication of the kind of treatment that they could expect from the captors in the days and weeks to come.

Almost immediately after arriving at Changi Barracks the prisoners were ordered to build a perimeter fence around the camp and then to sign a 'no escape form' which as Charles recalls was a major bone of contention:

> Army regulations forbid anybody taken prisoner to sign such a form. You should only give your name and rank to an enemy and our officers told us not to sign. Everybody was then forced to assemble on the Selarang Square in the barracks and remain there. Although this was a large square, when you consider that there were about 13,000 of us herded together in there, you can imagine what the conditions were like. Latrines had to be dug, and a few tents erected for those who needed some form of cover, but for most, including myself, we just stood, or slept, out in the open where we were. By this time many were beginning to suffer from dysentery, malaria and other diseases brought on by the poor food that we had been given since our capture. All the British food had been used up much earlier on and all we had to eat was brown rice that had been treated to preserve it, making it taste horrible. At length our officers realised that if we were to be left out on the barrack square for much longer, the subsequent loss of life could well be appalling. So we were told to sign the document under duress and were then allowed by our captors back into the barracks.

Towards the end of 1942 rumours had begun to spread that a railroad for military purposes was urgently needed in Burma and that the PoWs were to be transported from Changi (Singapore) to Banpong in Thailand where they were to be set to work building the railway. The railway was to be built between Nong Pladuk and the Three Pagodas Pass on the Burmese border, a distance of more than 400 kilometres. It would have to pass through miles of jungle and mountainous terrain following the course of the River Kwai. Charles recalled the horrendous rail journey north adding that beforehand the Japanese had assured everyone that they were being sent to a wonderful Red Cross camp in the cooler regions of Thailand:

> We were sent off in lorries to Singapore station and then loaded into cattle trucks (30–40 men to a wagon) for the five-day journey. And because the trucks were covered with metal sheeting the scorching heat of the day made conditions inside almost unbearable. The problem was that because we were packed in so tightly it was difficult to avoid touching the metal sheeting which became so hot under the mid-day sun. And following the intense heat of the

> day, the nights were extremely cold and all we had to cover us was a single blanket, having been told to leave our kit behind at Changi. Neither was it possible to lie down because of the dysentery, urine and sweat which made the atmosphere inside the trucks unbearable. We were fed just twice a day – morning and evening – with our meal consisting of just a small portion of rice or occasionally a little watery stew.

Charles and the other prisoners eventually arrived at Banpong on 3 November and after a short stay in a terribly flooded camp were forced to endure a torturous march (with further savage beatings for those who couldn't keep up) through the jungle for four days and three nights before arriving in the area where they were to be set to work:

> We eventually arrived at a place called Tarsao and our first job was to build a camp of huts about 400 feet above the river. At the same time we were set to work on the railway. Camp building, of course, was not part of the railway project so building the camp was considered a do-it-yourself leisure activity after a long day of exhausting work. Everything to do with the railway had to done by hand, whether it was felling trees through the jungle or cutting through the mountains of soil and rock with a pick and shovel. Our day began at seven in the morning when we were given a tin of rice for our breakfast. We were then given a further portion to take with us into the jungle to eat later. Our first job on arrival would be to find a spot out of the sun where we could leave our tins before starting work. Unfortunately, by lunch time most of the tins would be swarming with ants. So you either ate the rice as it was, tried to pick out as many ants as you could, or simply threw it all away. However, after a few days of going without you were happy to eat anything.
>
> The heat of the sun when working on the cuttings was unbearable as there was no cover whatsoever. By this time we had Japanese engineers and Korean guards who took great delight in taking it out on us PoWs. Anybody who did something that the Japanese thought was wrong was forced to stand outside the guard hut holding a rock, or a heavy piece of wood above their heads in the full sun until they collapsed and dropped to the floor. Another vile trick of theirs was to place a piece of goula malacca on the unfortunate person's head. When the treacly substance melted and trickled down his back, it attracted a particular variety of red ant that had a terrible bite. And then when they collapsed in agony the guard would kick and beat them in an attempt to make them stand again.

By the early months of 1943 Charles was suffering badly from dysentery and leg ulcers, and with hardly any medication available he was lucky to have avoided the fate of many who had to have their legs amputated in order to stop gangrene setting in. His weight had also plummeted to less than eight stone and without the efforts of some of the camp doctors (who at last were beginning to receive some Red Cross medicines) he would probably not have survived.

Things continued in a similar vein for the next two years with all the men suffering from continual bouts of dysentery, malaria and various other problems, while forever being moved to new locations as the railway progressed towards its final destination. At length, on 16 August 1945, and whilst making their way to the railway workings to begin yet another day's gruelling labour, Charles and his comrades were stopped by their guards and told to sit down and rest. Imagine their surprise when the Japanese then started handing out cigarettes – had they all gone mad they wondered! Charles recalled that one of his sergeants then went to the front of the party, which consisted of about 700 British, Dutch, Australian and American PoWs, and made an announcement:

> He climbed on top of this boulder and shouted out, 'Something has happened. You are all to go back to camp, but remember who you are.' When we arrived back in camp we were summoned to the parade ground by the sound of a British

Mary Jones, Charles's widow, with a map showing where he was incarcerated during the time of his captivity. The Author

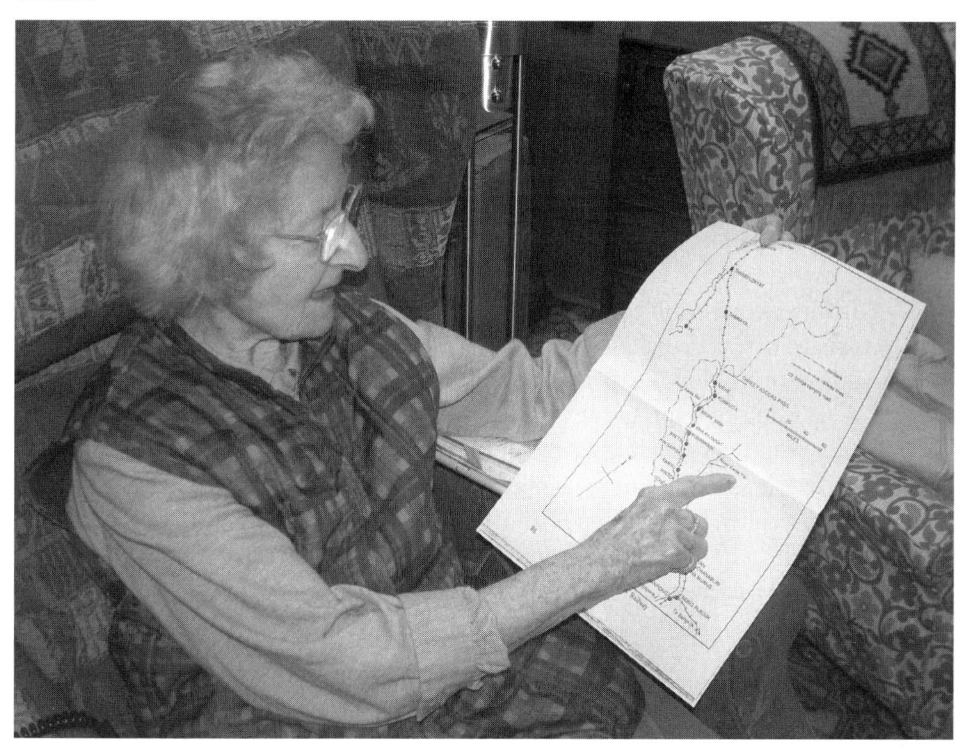

泰 4422 泰 IV ~~4422~~ 1485

收容所 Camp	~~馬来~~ 泰 昭和 年 月 日	番號 No.	~~馬来~~ 3,469
姓名 Name	JONES, CHARLES REGINALD.	生年月日 Date of Birth	1918.12.23.
國籍 Nationality	British 英	所属部隊 Unit	No. 902312 118th Field Regt.RA. ARMY
階級身分 Rank	LANCE BOMBARDIER 兵		
捕獲場所 Place of Capture	Singapore 昭南	捕獲年月日 Date of Capture	昭和 17 年 2 月 15 日
父ノ名 Father's Name	ROBERT CHARLES	母ノ名 Mother's Name	BEATRICE LOUISE
本籍地 Place of Origin	CATFORD, LONDON	職業 Occupation	Clerk 書記
通報先 Destination of Report	MR. ROBERT CHARLES JONES, 77, PERRY HILL, CATFORD, LONDON S.E.6	特記事項 Remarks	

Charles's Japanese PoW record card. Mary Jones collection

bugle call – which to us was a wonderful sound after being so used to hearing the Japanese one. And when we had all assembled, a sergeant-major mounted the podium and said, 'The war for us is over. Go and eat the meal that has been prepared for you, and on no account go anywhere near the Japanese.' And the scene that followed will always remain in the memories of those of us who were assembled there on that memorable day. Each group, in turn, proceeded to sing their national anthem. Tears were streaming down their faces and then we concluded with a rendering of *Land of Hope and Glory*.

What a delight it was the next day to stand by and watch the Dakota aircraft fly over with men standing by the open doors, ready to offload containers of goods by parachute. I can remember rushing over to one container that had burst open after being dropped and finding a tube of toothpaste. I rubbed the contents across my teeth savouring the delicious peppermint flavour. This incident may seem stupid now, but after existing on a diet of insipid rice, this was sheer bliss.

About a week later Charles was flown on to Rangoon where he and his companions were surprised to see a fleet of ambulances waiting to take them to their new camp. Later in the day as they were walking back along the road to their tents, a large car pulled up alongside and occupant got out and asked them to gather round:

> It was Lord Mountbatten. He said, 'Gather round chaps. I want you all to muster at the hospital steps.' So we did as requested and he stood over us and said, 'The Japanese are not invincible. An atom bomb has been dropped on Japanese territory and they have capitulated. We had a huge force waiting to attack the Japanese mainland but they were not needed.' He then wished us good luck and told us that transport would be arranged to get us home as soon as possible.
>
> We finally left for the long voyage home on the hospital ship *Worcestershire* and eventually arrived home in Liverpool. Some of the men had relatives waiting for them on the dockside and they were visibly shocked when they saw the amputees and badly wounded disembark. We then travelled by train to Paddington station and I was taken straight to a waiting Red Cross ambulance. Unbeknown to me, my brother had been waiting for me at the train barrier and I missed him. But I shall always remember arriving home at our garden gate and seeing my dear mother and father walking down the path to greet me, with tears of joy streaming down their faces.

A staff photograph from East Ward School in 1968. Charles is seated in the front on the extreme left. Author's collection

Charles Jones passed away in December 2002 at the age of eighty-three. His widow, Mary (to whom he was married for 55 years), continues to look back with pride on her husband's former military career. After returning home from the war Charles decided to enter the teaching profession and he will be remembered by many local people who were taught by him at either East Ward or Sir Charles Lucas Schools in Colchester.

CHAPTER 4

EVENTS

Oyster Lovers Come Out of Their Shells

One of the highlights of Colchester's social calendar is the prestigious annual Oyster Feast, a much publicised affair which is held in the Town Hall. The event is hosted by the Mayor of the day, whose prime responsibility is to send out invitations to between 300 or 400 local worthies, which will often include the names of one or two national celebrities. In recent years, for example, special guests have included the actor and comedian Warren Mitchell (of Alf Garnett fame), Jeremy Spake (from the *Airport* television programme), George Melly, Clive Anderson, Sandy Gall and so the list goes on. Each year, the identity of these special guests is kept very much under wraps, despite the odd attempt by some to glimpse a sneak preview of the menu card and toast list! (see later).

Sorting out oysters for the feast in 1910. Colchester Museums

Mayor Bill Harper helps to haul aboard the first catch of oysters during the 1931 season. Author's collection

The origin of the Oyster Feast is very much shrouded in mystery. Nothing much is known of its early beginnings, other than the fact that Colchester has always been famous for its oysters and that from ancient times there has been a strong tradition of corporate banqueting at various times of the year, where local oysters (Colchester Natives) would no doubt have formed part of the menu. The cultivation of oysters locally certainly pre-dates the coming of the Romans and, interestingly, shells of Colchester Natives have been discovered in Rome itself by modern-day archaeologists, suggesting that they were favoured by the Romans who exported them back to their homeland.

The earliest documented evidence which may relate to the start of the modern event is found in the Chamberlain's Accounts for 1667. Here we read that, '2 hole barrells and 4 halfs of oysters' were 'sent up by Mr Mayor's orders' at a cost to the town of sixteen shillings. A further two shillings was paid for, '2 case knifes' and six shillings, 'for the carriage of oysters.' The event became known as the Corporation Luncheon or Oyster Supper and until the 1840s was attended only by borough officials. It was not until 1845, when Alderman Henry Wolton became Mayor, that invitations to the event were extended to the wider public. The guest list for that year included some 200 names and for the first time the event was moved to the newly built Town Hall. Subsequent Mayors followed Alderman Wolton's example, and by 1887 the feast had outgrown the Town Hall and was moved to the new Corn Exchange.

One particular feature of the event, which has been taken up by successive Mayors from around this period, was the introduction of pictorial menu cards and toast lists. These have been produced in all shapes and sizes but usually incorporate some form of colourful artwork depicting various aspects of the town's historic past. The late Sir Gurney Benham was particularly adept at this and produced a whole range of humorous cartoon images for a succession of Oyster Feasts prior to his death in 1944.

The design of the card is usually left to the Mayor's discretion (within certain traditional guidelines) and may feature images connected with the Mayor's own background or place

Mayor Gurney Benham proclaims the oyster fishery open in 1908. Jean Blowers collection

The front of a menu card, drawn by Councillor Gurney Benham, for the 1899 Oyster Feast. Jean Blowers collection

The 1896 Oyster Feast at the Corn Exchange, formerly next to the Town Hall. Author's collection

The 1978 Oyster Feast in the Town Hall. Author's collection

of residence. For example, in 1994, the then Mayor, Tony Webb, included references to his home village of Tiptree, as well as his three children, on the design of the card.

One thing which can be relied upon, however, particularly if past Oyster Feasts are anything to go by, is that the first item on the menu will always feature Native Pyefleet Oysters served with brown bread and butter and washed down with a glass of Guinness.

Special Memories of Christmas Past

For most people today, Christmas is a time for high spending, fun and merriment. It is a time to relax and get together with family and friends and, usually, to eat far more than what is good for us. But this rush on spending and personal indulgence is a far cry from the way in which most families celebrated the festive season a hundred years ago – or even fifty years ago. In fact, as late the 1960s, the run up to Christmas was still much more traditional without most of the modern-day commercial trappings. In this short study of the occasion, and with the help of some fascinating personal memories, we will look back to see how Christmas was celebrated by many people during the early years of the last century.

Our story begins on Christmas Day of 1902, when a new initiative took place that was to bring a little festive cheer to hundreds of children from the poorer families of the town. The event was dubbed the 'Poor Children's Christmas Breakfast' and was held in the town's Corn Exchange. Nearly 1,000 children from around the town had been invited to attend. At 9 o'clock on Christmas morning they settled down at dozens of tables and tucked in to a grand 'breakfast' treat; and despite the early hour of the occasion, the menu reflected a typical party atmosphere. Hot meat pies, scones, current buns, cakes and sandwiches were eagerly devoured before being washed down with gallons of tea and cocoa. Following the meal the children each received some fruit, sweets and a new penny.

The event was the brainchild of Geoffrey Elwes, the son of the Mayor of the day, and who was later to become a leading light in the local Scouting movement. In fact, the breakfast, which was to be repeated annually for the next thirty-six years, became a major event in the annual Scouting calendar with all kinds of pre-event fundraising taking place throughout the year, as well as many Scouts turning up on the day itself to serve at tables. One such helper was Hector Free (born 1903) who was a member of the 1st Colchester Scout Troop:

> Every year several hundred children from all the schools in the town were entertained to a Christmas breakfast. I never had a Christmas at home for about twenty or thirty years of my life. The breakfast was held in the Corn Exchange and we used to have to go the previous evening, on Christmas Eve, and set out all the tables. Then on the Christmas morning we would go and serve out the meals.

Another helper at the event for several years running was Ethel Appleby (born 1901) who, during the 1930s, worked as head waitress for Last's restaurant in the High Street:

> They used to invite all the poor children of the town to breakfast at the Corn Exchange on Christmas morning, and our firm often got the job of organising it. That meant going in on Christmas Eve and helping to set out all the tables and equipment that would be needed. The next morning I had to put my own Christmas on hold to go to the Corn Exchange. The Children always had a hot meat pie – Last's used to make them. And then there would be brown bread and butter, scones, cakes and usually a jelly. Mr Last used to make the cocoa in three large portable coppers in the yard at the back of the Corn Exchange, slowly stirring the contents with broomstick handles. During the morning several visitors would arrive, including the mayor and mayoress, and there would be a band and various singsongs. The children were each given an apple and orange and a copper or two to take home. I used to get home at about 11.30 just in time to start on my own Christmas dinner.

Although most families during the inter-war years, and the earlier period, were very poor by modern standards, it would seem that only the most deserving of cases were given tickets to attend the breakfast. One such person was Margaret Dolby (born 1901) who had fond memories of the occasion:

The Poor Children's Christmas Breakfast in 1922. Ken Free collection

> The first Christmas after my father died us kids were given tickets to go the Christmas Breakfast. It was for poor children only, and we were poor – there's no doubt about it. We had mince pies and all that sort of thing – for breakfast! And when we came out we were all given an apple and a brand new penny.

Emily Daldry (born 1906) also attended the event on one occasion, but recalls never being allowed to go again:

> On one occasion when we were very young we went to the Christmas Breakfast for the children of working people. But when my father found out that a policeman was on duty there who lived near us, he wouldn't let us go again because he was ashamed.

Jack Ashton (born 1902) could also remember attending:

> In my younger days I used to attend the Poor Children's Breakfast at the Corn Exchange because I was one of the poor. I went with my brother Charlie and we had a nice breakfast. There would be hundreds of other children there and we ate whatever they dished up. After the breakfast we would be given an orange and apple and a bag of sweets which came from Hancock's in St Botolph's Street.

The last Children's Breakfast took place in 1938, just before the Second World War, although by this time the event had become known as simply The Children's Breakfast, the word 'poor' having been omitted. On this occasion, numbers attending were severely reduced owing to the bad weather and infantile paralysis prevailing in some parts of the town. Nevertheless, the event went ahead as planned with those present tucking into the usual fare of hot meat pies, scones and current buns etc. As usual, the Mayor and Mayoress (on this occasion Councillor and Mrs Handy Fisher) arrived during the proceedings and made a tour of the tables talking to the children.

Jack Ashton who used to attend the Poor Children's Breakfast at the Corn Exchange. The Author

The annual Christmas Breakfast would no doubt have brought some happiness to many children who might otherwise have

Christmas Day in the Children's Ward at Essex County Hospital, 1938, with children dressed up as Snow White and the Seven Dwarfs. Graham Fisher collection

had very little to cheer about. But for most people of the time, poor or otherwise, Christmas was a vastly different affair to that experienced by the majority of people today, particularly with regard to the kind of presents received by the children.

Phyllis Gibbons (born 1915) recalled a typical Christmas morning from her childhood days:

> We used to hang our stockings up and would perhaps get an orange, a few nuts and maybe a threepenny bit or some coppers. We used to decorate the home with paper chains and we once had a tree. We always had a family Christmas and would have a chicken – one that had been reared in the back garden. It was the best that we could afford.

Joe Lawrence (born 1903) recalled that there was always a lot of food on the table at Christmas, but his mother had to save up all year for it:

> There was more meat in our house at Christmas than there was in a butchers shop. It was open house, all the family was there. The house was decorated. Mum used to buy strips of paper and we would make chains with paste made out of flour. We also used to have a tree – no lights or anything like that and the only presents we got was an apple, orange, nuts and a penny in a stocking. Mum would be up at about three or four in the morning on Christmas Day making jam tarts and sausage rolls, and we would come down and ask whether Father

> Christmas had been. The day was then spent mostly eating and drinking and singing songs. Boxing Day was mother's day – she did nothing. That day you looked after yourself and it was her rest day.

Regardless of the financial limitations, Christmas was generally a happy time, an opportunity to get together with friends and relatives, and to even venture into the almost sacrosanct front room of the house which throughout the year would rarely have been used. Joan Reynolds (born 1922) recalls some of the fun and games that used to take place on Christmas Day at her family home:

> My mother had nine brothers and sisters who all got married and we used to go to each other's houses all over Christmas. We used to play games and that until one or two o'clock in the morning. We played Postman's Knock, Come and See the Sultan and many others. We used to have a singsong and carols, but nobody ever got drunk. I remember we had a fire one year at my uncle's house. My dad's younger brother used to go in for decorations in a big way and this particular year he had done it like a cave under the sea. There were streamers all across the ceiling and cotton wool and fairy lights. I had taken my younger brother Ronnie down there and they said to take him through to see the lights. Well when he switched them on all this cotton wool went up and there was pandemonium for a few minutes – it was dropping on everybody. Little Ronnie ran down to the bottom of the garden and it took ages to get him back in the house. The next time we took him there he said, 'We're not going to play that game again are we?'

Raging Torrent Brings Chaos and Disaster

Despite the increasing frequency of damage from heavy rain and flooding in our communities, nothing can compare with the catastrophe that descended upon the region over half a century ago, bringing death and destruction in its path. This, of course, was The Great Storm of Saturday 31 January 1953, which resulted in some of the worst flooding in living memory along the eastern coast of England.

For the people of Essex, this was indeed a black mark in the county's history with 119 lives claimed and 13,000 people evacuated from their homes. The worst affected areas in terms of human casualties were the coastal communities of Canvey Island, Jaywick and Harwich, where more than a hundred people (a third of all drownings reported in the country) lost their lives. But such was the force of the storm and tidal surge that all communities located along the tidal river systems were affected.

Alice Farthing from Colchester remembered being woken in the early hours of the morning by an unusual noise in her bedroom:

The riverside villages of Wivenhoe and Rowhedge (far side) bore the brunt of the rising tide waters (1953?). Andrew Phillips collection

My husband and I were living in a couple of downstairs rooms in Hythe Station Road and on this particular morning I heard this strange knocking noise in our bedroom. It turned out that our bed was afloat and was knocking on the bedroom wall, and when my husband went to get out of bed he found himself up to his waist in water.

The submerged quayside at Wivenhoe. Glen Jackson collection

Hawkins Road in Colchester and the adjoining Lathe Company car park were completely covered in flood water.
Andrew Phillips collection

Jack Austin, who was living near the waterfront at Rowhedge, also had vivid recollections of waking up on the morning of the flood:

> The water was right up to the gates. So I got my sea boots on, climbed the fence, unlocked the gates and led a couple of horses out which had been standing in water all night.

By far the worst memories of the event, however, are those recalled by people who were living nearer to the coast in places such as Jaywick, near Clacton, where thirty-seven people were drowned. This small holiday resort comprising nearly 2,000 holiday chalets and bungalows was in a state of complete turmoil. By 1.45 am on Sunday morning, the sea wall on the St Osyth side of the resort had been breached in a number of places, allowing millions of gallons of sea water to pour across the marshes towards the back of Jaywick. The community was now trapped between this raging torrent and the full force of the sea at the front and within minutes most of the community had been flooded in up to eight feet of water. The water rose so fast that many victims were simply drowned in their beds. For others, alerted to the impending disaster, it was a frantic scramble to secure some high ground, in some cases by literally smashing their way into the roof space of their homes through the ceiling.

One such couple were John and Mary Reeves, who were warned of the approaching danger by disabled neighbour Marie Miles. Mary remembered the frantic struggle they had to get their children to safety:

> I jumped out of bed and put my feet straight into the water. My husband lifted the children up into the loft and we just sat up there singing and telling the children stories because we didn't want them to hear the people screaming. We stayed there until one of the flood men came in and got us out through the window and took us up the road in a boat.

Unfortunately, one of those drowned was Marie Miles, who being paralysed from the waist down was unable to escape the eight foot high wall of water in her home.

The next morning help was on hand from the police, the military and civilians alike as they took part in an intense search for survivors. One of these 'flood men' as so described by Mary Reeves, was Peter Wright, who at the time was a twenty-six-year-old living in nearby Clacton. Peter recalls that he and a couple of colleagues were stopped by the police as they tried to enter Jaywick the following morning:

> I was completely dumfounded because until I saw the water I didn't even know that there had been a flood. I told them that my family lived in Jaywick and that I worked there, but they said, 'I'm sorry but you can't come through because we're rescuing people. The only way that you will get in to Jaywick is to go back to Clacton and walk along the sea wall.' So this is what we did. As it turned out our piece of Jaywick wasn't too badly affected but we stayed on there for most of the day helping out the local police constable, Harry Mitchell, with the rescue work. A friend of mine, Jimmy the milkman, and I got a dingy and rowed up and down the roads looking for survivors. Being the local milkman, Jimmy knew where all the elderly people lived, so we started off by rowing down Meadow Way to the home of

Peter Wright who helped in the rescue effort at Jaywick. EADT

Rescuers at work helping people to escape from their homes in Jaywick. EADT

> a Mr and Mrs Drew. Unfortunately they had drowned and I had never seen drowned people before – and it's not nice. Mr Drew had apparently collapsed and died whilst trying to escape though the bathroom window. We had to lift his body over the bath from where he had fallen in the water, which by this time was about four feet deep. His wife had died in her bed, but when we got to her body it was half submerged on the floor in the water. We didn't have to lift her – we just sort of floated her out. We then towed their bodies behind the dingy towards an area where the water wasn't quite so deep and then put their bodies into the van. From there, they were taken up to the Café Morocco, where PC Mitchell tied a label around their necks and put them on a stretcher before they were taken away.

Harwich was another town which bore the brunt of the storm. Shortly after 9 pm, the harbour master had noticed that the tide had reached high water level over three hours ahead of time, and was rising fast. By midnight the quay, the esplanade and the Bathside area were under water. The water then surged into the town centre

PC Taffy Bateman former Colchester Borough Police.
Author's collection

flooding gardens and basements. Eventually the whole main street, from the quay to the police station was under several feet of water. Taffy Bateman, a retired police constable from Colchester, remembered receiving a message over his car radio to report to Harwich:

> We were on patrol at the time and we got this message over the radio to report at once to Harwich. When we got to the police station there and looked down the road towards the sea, we saw this big shiny black patch in the middle of the road – it was the top of the doctor's car. We spent several nights after that down at Jaywick patrolling round to stop any people trying to get in the houses and doing any damage or looting.

The local water board was also at full stretch trying to reduce the risk of contamination in the mains. Jim Lee, who worked for the Colchester Water Board, remembers being sent down to Harwich to assist in organising some emergency chlorination work:

> Those in the Tendring Hundred area were in a lot trouble. The water flooded large areas of Harwich immersing kitchens and taps in sea water. We went down there and set up operations at the Dovercourt water tower, where we tried to inject chlorine into the pipework supplying the Parkeston and Bathside areas. At the same we had gangs of men going round the houses equipped with goggles and gloves and bleach powder, which they mixed up into the size of a golf ball before ramming it up the spout of every tap that was still visible. This was the only way we could think of sterilising the taps which, of course, had been covered by the water. We also had vans going round saying 'Don't use the water' because we didn't know how far it had reached.

After the flooding came the inevitable clean-up operation. As the waters subsided, the devastation caused by the flooding became all too evident. At Jaywick, some bungalows and chalets had been completely upended and tossed some distance from their original site. At the very least, the contents of the houses affected had been swamped and badly damaged by the water, which itself had left behind a thick layer of mud and slime in its wake.

And so, despite our present day worries and problems with localised flooding, thankfully the risks to life itself remain fairly minimal. The Great Storm of 1953 will no doubt be remembered for many years to come, but fingers crossed, never again repeated.

Celebrating a Proud History

For many years the highlight of Colchester's social calendar was the annual Carnival parade and Military Tattoo. Crowds of people would converge on the town centre to enjoy an action-packed hour or so as carnival floats of all descriptions would wend their through the town's historic streets. Then, of course, there was the added bonus of the brilliant Military Tattoo – one of the largest in Europe – which was held on Lower Castle Park. It was all part of a busy week of fun and merriment which gave everyone something to cheer about. Sadly, however, as with most good things, it came to a regrettable end in the 1990s, and in February 2005 the Colchester Community Fund, the group responsible for staging the events since the early 1950s, was finally dissolved. But the group's fifty-three year history is a proud one and the memories of those people directly involved in bringing so much enjoyment to the local community tell the story of those special times.

Massed bands on Lower Castle Park. Colchester Community Fund

The Colchester Community Fund was formed towards the end of 1951, primarily to raise funds for local causes. The impetus to form the group, however, was also partly due to the highly successful Festival of Britain which had been celebrated across the country earlier in the year, and particularly in Colchester where a week of activities had included the presentation of a play written especially for the occasion by Dorothy L Sayers, at the Playhouse.

By 1954, it had been decided to revive the old Colchester Carnival, an event which had existed before the war to raise money for the local hospital. This included a procession through the streets and two evening events in the Castle Park. The programme included displays by the Castle Motorcycling Club, football and baseball matches, a wild west show, various marching bands and a small torchlight tattoo followed by fireworks. There were also plenty of side shows for the public's entertainment including horse racing, darts, catch the rat, bagatelle and roll-a-penny.

Over the next few years a similar range of events were staged, although year by year the organisers became a little bolder and incorporated such attractions as a steam traction engine rally, grass track motorcycle championships and even athletics. The next major change to the proceedings came in 1960 when the chairman of the Fund, David Papillon, made an approach to the Garrison Commander asking whether they would be interested in staging a proper military tattoo. This they readily agreed to and Major Philip Crutchfield was given the job of producing it. He recalls that he had no previous experience of staging such an event, but knew that he would have to put on some kind of display. And as it turned out things didn't go quite according to plan:

> We had plenty of soldiers to hand and we decided to divide them into two groups – the goodies and the baddies – and in order to give the occasion some kind of reality we decided to let off some smoke – a common tactic in warfare when you want to hide movements of troops. Well we put up a whole lot of smoke and it was a complete disaster, because the smoke just hung there, it wouldn't go away. I as commentator couldn't see what I was supposed to be commentating on, the audience couldn't see what was going on, and worse still the troops couldn't see what was going on either. But happily the smoke eventually lifted and we were able to continue.

From this time on the Tattoo became a regular feature of the Carnival celebrations and the programme would often feature guest bands from various foreign regiments, including members of the Hong Kong Police Force, the Lion Dancers from Singapore and on one occasion the Royal Canadian Mounted Police who performed their famous 'Musical Walk.' The events were also used by the Army to encourage people to join the service and various recruiting tents and side shows were always on hand. On one occasion they even rigged up a tall tower where visitors could experience a parachute landing with the help of a special harness and winch.

It had also become a regular feature to open the Tattoo with a special flypast by RAF Phantom or Falcon jets, which would come screaming across the arena at low level, much to the delight, and at times the surprise, of the crowd. In fact, they would come in so low and fast that they would often set off numerous car and burglar alarms in the area. The fly past itself would then be followed by a team of parachutists, who having leapt from a high flying Hercules or Beverley aircraft, would endeavour to land in the centre of the arena. However, once again things didn't always go quite according to plan as recalled by David Snow, a Community Fund member since the mid 1950s:

> In the early days, before the advent of modern controllable parachutes where they can virtually pinpoint their landing area, they would sometimes miss the arena altogether. I can remember one occasion when a member of the parachute team actually landed on top of a café roof in Lion Walk in the centre of town.

Another Community Fund member who has several stories to tell of events relating to the Tattoo is Westley Sandford, a founding member of the group and its Chairman for the last twenty-eight years. When asked which Tattoo he remembered the most vividly he had no hesitation in recalling one particular performance in 1968:

David Snow, Community Fund member since the 1950s. The Author

Westley Sandford, Chairman and founding member of the Colchester Community Fund. Westley Sandford collection

> It had been a little wet and one of the motorcycle team fell off and broke his leg and then during one of the displays a horse also broke its leg near the main entrance. Well we managed to get the horse out of the arena but it was so badly injured that it had to be put down. Sadly, after it had been shot its body could still be seen every time we opened the main gate and so in true army fashion they got a body of men to stand in front of the dead horse so that it couldn't be seen from the grandstand. One of these men standing in front of the horse was a cockney gentleman and was heard to say in a loud voice, 'The one good thing about a dead horse is that it looks like a dead horse.' What he didn't realise was that he had said this in the hearing of the horse's rider and he was subsequently taken to hospital with a broken jaw! And then to cap it all one of the helicopters came in on a new route and flew directly over the NAFFI tent and the air was full of crisps and crisp packets, and the manager was scolded with his own tea.

By the early 1980s security was becoming something of a problem, particularly in the Castle Park where there were so many public access points. And then, following a spate of terrorist attacks elsewhere in the UK, the police and military authorities were becoming

A member of the Royal Artillery parachute display team lands safely in the Tattoo arena. EADT

David Judge from the Colchester Community Fund. EADT

very concerned about security. In 1984 the event was moved to the Abbey Field, where it continued on a biennial basis until its final performance in 1990. Although there have been attempts to produce one or two similar events with fewer military participants they failed to attract enough public support. In the town centre the carnival too was suffering setbacks. Although the traditional Carnival parade was to continue for a few more years, new requirements from the police to provide proper barriers to hold back the crowds was a request too far. The sheer cost of providing such equipment would have been in excess of any monies collected on the day, and this together with rising insurance premiums and other expenses, was turning the whole event into a loss making exercise.

In February 2005, having raised nearly half a million pounds over the previous fifty-three years, and with membership at an all time low, the organisers of the Colchester Community Fund finally decided to call it a day. To mark the occasion a special farewell presentation was hosted by the Mayor of Colchester, Councillor John Bouckley, in the Town Hall. Invites to attend the event were extended to the five surviving members of the Community Fund (Westley Sandford, David Judge, Chris Dowsett, Bernard Johnson and Dennis Marchant), who were joined by about sixty others who had supported the group over the years.

The evening was chaired by Community Fund member David Judge who had arranged for some key people to speak about their special memories. It had also been agreed that whatever funds were remaining in the kitty would go towards a commemorative bench in the Castle Park. At the time of the reception, however, Jackie Bowis, on behalf of King Cole's Kittens (an offshoot of the community fund of which the late Bill Tucker was a leading light) announced that they too would be donating a seat for the park. The evening then concluded with the arrival of Lance Corporal Barry Ryall of the Parachute Regiment Band who played the *Last Post* – a fitting end to fifty-three years of fund raising.

CHAPTER 5

TRANSPORT

Take Public Transport on a Trip Down Memory Lane

Recent stories regarding the installation of a new tramway or cable car system in Colchester where we would all be whisked around in comparative ease, free from the stresses of modern life, may seem appealing, but do most people really want to travel by public transport? Regardless of whether you love them or loath them, most of today's generation would probably be very reluctant to abandon their cars in favour of a more reliable public transport system. They would rather put up with the congested roads and resulting pollution rather than lose the freedom that their cars afford them. It's a problem, of course, that can only get worse and will ultimately have to be dealt with – but what about life in the past? How, for example, did the generation of a hundred years ago get around.

Well in 1900, for example, motorised transport was still very much in its infancy and the sight of a motor car trundling its way through the town would have been a rare one. The electric tramway system had also yet to make its appearance, and as far as public transport was concerned, the horse still reigned supreme. In fact, the early Edwardian period probably marked the high point of horse transport generally with some three or four million of them being employed on the nation's roads.

In Colchester, at this time, the main form of public transport was the horse-drawn hackney carriage, which of course was the forerunner of our modern taxi. Indeed, the records show that, in 1901, there were some 115 licensed horse cabs operating in the town, the majority of which were a type known as a brougham which was a four-wheeled carriage drawn by a single horse, and which could accommodate up to four passengers. Fares were quite expensive with most journeys costing anything between sixpence and a shilling (2½–5p) a mile, which was a little beyond the budgets of most ordinary folk, at least as far as using the cabs on a regular basis was concerned.

The brougham was particularly favoured by older members of the public and family groups. Alice Twyman, born in 1906, was one who had fond memories of riding in a such a cab:

> My father often used to hire a brougham, or what he used to call a four-wheeler, to take us to the station when we were going on holiday from Siggers in

Horse cabs queue for business outside Colchester Town Hall in 1902. Author's collection

> Sir Isaac's Walk. The door of the cab was on the side and you would put your foot onto this metal ring and pull yourself up into the cab. Inside the cab, one seat would be back to the cabby and the other facing forward, so that two people would sit facing each other. The luggage would be put on top with the cabby.

The most popular of the smaller two-wheeled cabs at the time was the hansom, which on the streets of Colchester, ran a close second in popularity to the larger brougham. The hansom, however, was really a cab for the young and adventurous and, like the brougham, was drawn by a single horse. You entered the cab from the front through a pair of flap doors where there was room for two passengers sitting side by side. The hansom was also reckoned to be a much faster vehicle than the larger brougham and its solid rubber types ensured a smoother and quieter ride.

The horse cabbies themselves were bound by a stringent set of rules and regulations all of which had to be strictly adhered to. They were to obey a maximum speed limit of six miles per hour and smoking without the permission of their fare was forbidden. After every hiring the driver was required to make a diligent search of the carriage to check for lost property, and when lining up at one of the official cab ranks, of which there were four in Colchester, each carriage had to be facing in the same direction – in other words, they were not allowed to put two horse's heads together. Finally, the maximum distance to which a carriage could

The two-wheeled Hansom cab was popular with the people of Colchester. Author's collection

be drawn was just five miles, which effectively confined all journeys to within the borough limits. For those wanting to venture further afield, or travel to and from the country villages, the only other option was the carrier's cart.

Almost every village was served by at least one firm of carriers who, with their small covered-in carts, which were more akin to the wagons of the American Wild West, would make regular journeys into the larger towns. Their main income was derived from operating a kind of shopping, or fetch-and-carry service, for the local inhabitants, charging a small commission or fee for each errand completed, and in most cases providing space for a few fare-paying passengers. The carriers also operated a kind of early parcel post system whereby a package or parcel could be sent to almost any location you care to name via the extensive carrier network.

In 1901, there were over fifty such firms operating in and out of Colchester. Several would make the journey on a daily basis, some just once or twice a week, but almost universally on a Saturday, which was market day. On arriving in Colchester the carrier would stable his horse at one the local inns or hotels while he went around the town conducting his business. By late afternoon he would be back at the stable preparing his horse for the return journey, usually with half-a-dozen or so passengers crowded in the back of the cart. Frequent stops would be made along the way to drop off orders or parcels collected during the day.

Of course, for most of us, the concept of horse-drawn carriages and carrier carts being considered as a serious form of public transport is confined to the history books, something totally detached from our present way of life. But for a few individuals such thoughts still conjure up warm memories of days gone by. One such individual was Jack Austin, who as a sprightly ninety-four-year-old in 2001, must surely have been one of the last surviving local carriers. Jack began working with the Rowhedge carrier (Mr Fale) before he was old enough to leave school, and eventually went on to operate the business himself. He remembered that in the early days they were still using a horse to pull the cart:

Jack Austin, aged ninety-four, from Rowhedge. The Author

> We used to deliver parcels to and from town and to the clothing factories. Lots of people did tailoring then. We had just the one horse and cart to start with, and the cart was made of wood, like a square box. We later put that on a Ford chassis when we got rid of the horse. We used to charge about tuppence (2p) to take a parcel to town and we would also do shopping for people, especially during the First World War. We had to queue up, which took a long time and we'd be late home. If we had room, we would take passengers, perhaps two or three, but after a time, when the

C & E Moore's horse-drawn carrier cart pictured in the early 1900s. Author's collection

parcel deliveries died out, we took more. They would sit round the side on wooden seats – it wasn't very comfortable.

By the start of the First World War horse transport in the town was already in steep decline with many cab proprietors and carriers converting to motor vehicles. The electric tramway had also arrived on the scene in 1904 providing a much needed cheaper form of transport for the masses. As for the continued success and popularity of the motor car – well the rest is history.

Turning Tides of Ferry's Fortune

If you fancy doing something a little different during the summer months, and particularly if you like the idea of messing about on the water, then why not pop down to either Wivenhoe or Rowhedge and take a ride on the ferry. The ferry boat is operated on a part-time basis by the Wivenhoe Ferry Trust, and provides leisure trips to the three waterside communities of Wivenhoe, Rowhedge and Fingringhoe. The service is operated on a limited basis using volunteer crews and, to its credit, has been running for some fourteen years with passenger numbers rising steadily. This is not to say, of course, that the enterprise is a modern invention. On the contrary, until the 1950s and 1960s there was a permanent ferry service operating here which had probably been in existence for generations, providing a critical link across the river for both traders and the general public alike.

This is believed to be the Wivenhoe doctor returning from a call in Fingringhoe. Glen Jackson collection

The Wivenhoe ferryman, Arthur Bell, with his passengers (from left to right) Barry Eves, Mrs Coralie Summers and John Harris, c.1950s. Glen Jackson collection

Exactly when the ferry first started operating is not known but one would expect that river transport of some kind has been in evidence at this location for several hundred years. In fact, there were two ferries working this stretch of the river – the *Wivenhoe Ferry* which crossed between Wivenhoe and Fingringhoe, the rights of which were owned by Colchester Borough Council, and the *Rowhedge Ferry* which operated between Rowhedge and Wivenhoe and which seems to have been operated independently. The earliest documented evidence of a ferry working here, however, is to be found in a diary belonging to Fingringhoe farmer Joseph Page who recorded the following comments in April 1800:

> Went and dined W. Simson's, Ardleigh. Could not get the colt into the ferry boat, was obliged to swim it through

And again just a few weeks later on 10 June, he wrote:

> The club dinner at the Rose and Crown, Wivenhoe. Sunday expenses, and at the club, gave ferryman for sitting up, 6s 6d.

The ferry in question was probably the Wivenhoe Ferry and although Page neglects to mention how much he had to pay for the crossing, he does note giving the ferryman a sizeable tip for 'sitting up'. On the face of it, this seems to have been a little on the generous side and may well have been equal to the ferryman's entire earnings for the day. This can be surmised from a lease drawn up to operate the ferry by Colchester Borough Council in 1926 when the fare for a foot passenger travelling on the ferry between the hours of 6 am and 9 pm was fixed at one halfpenny, increasing to one penny between 9–10 pm. And if the ferryman was obliged to turn out during the night to ferry the doctor across the river he was still only able to claim one shilling – much less than the payment given by farmer Page well over a hundred years earlier.

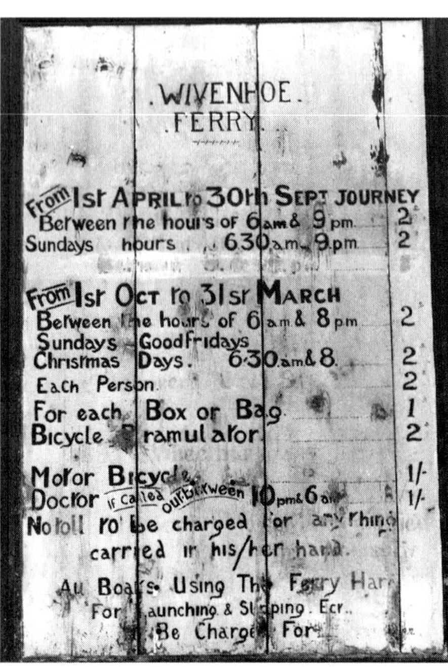

A list of toll charges for the Wivenhoe ferry. Glen Jackson collection

The schedule of tolls for 1926 makes no provision for the carrying of horses, but bicycles, perambulators, wheelbarrows and motorcycles were all allowed at a halfpenny apiece, except for the motorcycles which cost threepence. There was no toll or charge made for anything that was carried or held by the passenger in his or her hand. At certain times of the day, it might have been possible to paddle one's way across the river bed on what was a fairly hard gravel bottom. Horses that needed to make the journey across would almost certainly have gone by this latter route.

The records become much more abundant from the middle of the nineteenth century when we learn of a whole variety of people making regular use of the ferry. For instance, in *Kelly's Directory* for 1874 mention is made that the afternoon post from Colchester arrives at Rowhedge via Wivenhoe (presumably on the ferryboat). Milk in large metal churns was carried across the river on the ferryboat from Fingringhoe farms for sale in Wivenhoe, tradesmen from both sides of the water made the daily crossing to work in the shipyards and other industries, and many girls from Wivenhoe are known to have been employed over in the Rowhedge clothing factories. Also, as previously mentioned, the nearest doctor's surgery for those living in the Rowhedge or Fingringhoe area was at Wivenhoe, which either meant hopping on the ferry for the short trip across the river, or making a five or six mile detour via The Hythe at Colchester.

By the 1950s the ferry charges had risen to 2d for foot passengers and bicycles, plus a penny for any extra box or bag. The charge for carrying a motorcycle or for calling out the doctor at night remained at one shilling. However, by this time the long term future of the ferry was looking bleak. Local industry on both sides of the river had declined, and the ever-increasing popularity of the motor car was making personal travel that much easier and more convenient. The ferries struggled on for as long as they could but, by 1952,

Albert Payne, one of the Wivenhoe milkmen, waits on the far side of the river as the milk churns are loaded up on the Fingringhoe side. Glen Jackson collection

Day-trippers returning from Wivenhoe on the Rowhedge ferry, c.1955. Anon. *Rowhedge Recollections* 1977.

the ferryman operating the Wivenhoe Ferry was lucky if he got half-a-dozen customers a day, and the owners of the enterprise, Colchester Borough Council, decided to close it down in the September of that year. As might be expected, there was a local outcry demanding that the ferry be reopened. As a result, the ferry started up again for a short while the following year but finally succumbed on a permanent basis in November 1953 due to lack of support. Even then the local people did not concede defeat and, in 1955, a local parishioner instigated a High Court action in an attempt to force the Borough to reconsider. This resulted in the Lord Chief Justice, no less, who had himself visited the area, expressing his sympathy at the parishioners' plight, but at the same time deciding that the Council could not be forced to run a business at a loss, and so that was the end of the Wivenhoe Ferry. The Rowhedge Ferry struggled on until the late 1960s before it too finally closed.

For the next thirty or so years the communities drifted slowly apart until the ferry link had become all but a memory in the minds of some of the older members of the community. But then, in 1992, a group of volunteers decided to form the Wivenhoe Ferry Trust with the aim of re-establishing, albeit in a small way, this lifeline across the river. The result has been a huge success with participants from both sides of the river getting involved. At the present time (2005), the ferry operates at weekends and bank holidays throughout the summer months, according to the tides, and one can simply just turn up and hop on board – the cost is just £1 a trip. Or if you would like to plan something a little more adventurous, then the possibilities are endless. You could, for example, hire the boat (which holds up to ten people) for a special trip for your own enjoyment and perhaps enjoy a riverside picnic at nearby Alresford Creek, or perhaps stop at one of the waterside pubs for a drink and a meal.

A word of caution, however, is perhaps necessary at this juncture because you may discover that you like the experience so much that it becomes addictive! This appears to be the case concerning the Gibson-Hart family from Rowhedge. Paul Gibson-Hart tells me that he and his wife, Zoe, and daughters Anna and Ella, make use of the ferry service most weekends:

> We use the ferry to cross over to Wivenhoe on a fairly regular basis. We take the girls to the park and use the opportunity to visit my mother who still lives in Wivenhoe. The journey is, of course, much shorter than by using the road, but the main attraction for us is the river crossing which is something of a weekly adventure for my two daughters.

It is also, perhaps, worth relating one or two amusing incidents which have occurred since the service has been re-opened. The first concerns a Transit van from overseas which pulled up at the quayside at Wivenhoe. One of their number approached the ferry crew and asked how long it would take to get to Southend! The second experience relates to an American visitor who upon leaving Wivenhoe on the ferry, enquired of the crew and the other passengers, 'Hey guys, what's the weather going to be like in this here place we're heading for – Row Hedge?' Finally, and bearing in mind that the ferry is clearly marked

The modern ferry in operation in 1995. The Author

on the new ordnance survey maps, you can imagine the look of surprise on the faces of the crew when a holiday-maker turned up on the Fingringhoe side of the river in his car, towing a huge caravan, and expecting to be taken across the river to Wivenhoe.

Bus Journeys that were Just the Ticket

Anyone who has travelled on a modern-day coach will know that the experience can be quite a pleasant one – luxury seating, air-conditioning, television and sometimes even a built-in loo are all features that we have come to expect as standard. But, of course, it was a vastly different experience for those of earlier generations who had to endure the extremes of weather in open-top vehicles, a bumpy ride and, in some cases, be expected to actually get off the vehicle and walk up steep hills!

The first omnibus service to have been established in England was that started by George Shillibeer in 1829, who had seen similar vehicles plying the streets of Paris a few years earlier whilst working as a coach builder in the city. Upon returning home he decided to set up his own omnibus service, and designed and built a series of vehicles which were capable of seating up to twenty-two passengers on two rows of inward facing benches. The vehicles were staffed by professional coachmen in smart livery, and each bus was provided with cushions for passenger comfort, and newspapers and books for them to read during their journey. The experiment proved an instant success and, before long, he had a whole fleet of vehicles in service, each with the name *Shillibeer* emblazoned along the sides. The name became something of a trademark and people would speak of 'taking a Shillibeer' when travelling by bus.

A Shillibeer omnibus from the 1830s. Author's collection

Unfortunately for Mr Shillibeer, the venture was to prove so successful that he soon found himself competing with a number of jealous rivals, some of whom resorted to devious tactics in order to win his customers. For instance, one of their ploys was to paint the name Shillibeer on the side of their own buses, preceded by the words 'Not an Original' in minute lettering. And, of course, the would-be passenger who had rushed to jump on what they thought was a genuine Shillibeer, found that it was to late to get off when they realised that it didn't match up to their high expectations.

Many of Shillibeer's passengers also took away his books so that they could finish off a particular story, but then forgot to return them. And so after just six years of trading, Shillibeer was finally forced off the road and instead started up a funeral carriage service. Once again he had his name painted on the sides of his vehicles but, of course, people no longer liked to talk of 'taking a Shillibeer'.

By about 1845 it had become customary for some of the male passengers to climb onto the roof of the omnibuses, in order to complete their journey when there was no room below. And, in 1852, the first so-called 'Knife-board' omnibus had been established whereby a plank of wood was bolted to the top of the bus and people would sit here, back to back, facing the road, whilst leaning against the board. By this time, outside travel was even being encouraged by halving the cost of the ordinary fare.

A knife-board omnibus in London in the 1860s. Author's collection

By the 1860s a few daring ladies had also started to venture on to the roof seats and, in order to protect their decency, modesty or decency boards were fitted to the sides of the buses to shield the view – of their ankles! Before long some enterprising people started using the boards for advertising purposes. A typical knife-board omnibus could accommodate twenty-six passengers – twelve seated inside, ten on top and two seated either side of the driver. By the early 1880s a new style of vehicle had been developed, which was known as a 'Garden Seat' omnibus. Again, there was room for twelve passengers seated inside, with fourteen more, seated in pairs, facing the front, on the upper deck.

Outside of London and the major cities, the most popular type was the Station or Private omnibus. This model, which also operated in the towns and villages of Essex and Suffolk, dated from around the 1860s and provided accommodation for between six and eight passengers seated on inward-facing seats around the sides of the vehicle, plus one or two extra spaces up front with the driver.

Many of the older omnibus proprietors, particularly at a local level, actually started off with just a simple carrier's cart, providing local communities with a fetch and carry service to and from the nearest town. Local examples are Osborne's of Tollesbury, Hutley's of Coggeshall, Norfolk's of Nayland and Moore's of Kelvedon, the latter of which are able to trace its roots back to 1815, when the business began with a cart and three donkeys. Most of the old firms, however, started up their operations during the late 1800s, and converted to motor power in the early years of the twentieth century.

One of the first local firms to covert to motor power, indeed one of the first in the whole country, was Arthur Berry of Port Lane, Colchester, who, on Christmas Eve 1904, started a service travelling to and from Mersea Island. The bus was a Damiler and while Mr Berry senior did the driving, his young son Stanley collected the fares of 1/4d (7p) return. Young Stanley was just sixteen years old at the time but was soon driving the bus himself (officially that is) once he had passed his seventeenth birthday. In fact, he had been driving through the streets of Colchester in his father's tiller-steered Panhard (the second car in Colchester) from the age of fourteen but, as Stanley noted many years later, 'Things were a bit different then.' Stanley's job was to go down to The Hythe to collect petrol from the quayside which had arrived at the port by ship. Obviously there were no petrol stations in those days, and the railway was still refusing to transport anything of a highly flammable nature. In 1922, the firm added Brightlingsea to its route and continued plying between the two destinations until being taken over by the Eastern National Omnibus Company in 1937.

Another familiar site on the streets of Colchester, from around the 1920s, was the fleet of Silver Queen buses, which served the coastal districts of the Tendring Hundred. The buses were typical of the period, having open tops, solid rubber tyres and acetylene lamps for lighting. And, as one might expect, they could be quite difficult to drive, with gear changing being particularly awkward until the engine oil had warmed up. In the days when all engines had to be cranked by hand, starting up first thing on a cold morning was particularly difficult

An assortment of early buses lined up in the old St John's Street bus station in 1926. Their destinations included such places as Halstead, Tiptree, Chelmsford, Maldon and Braintree. Author's collection

Silver Queen buses standing outside the Hippodrome Theatre in Colchester High Street, c.1921. Author's collection

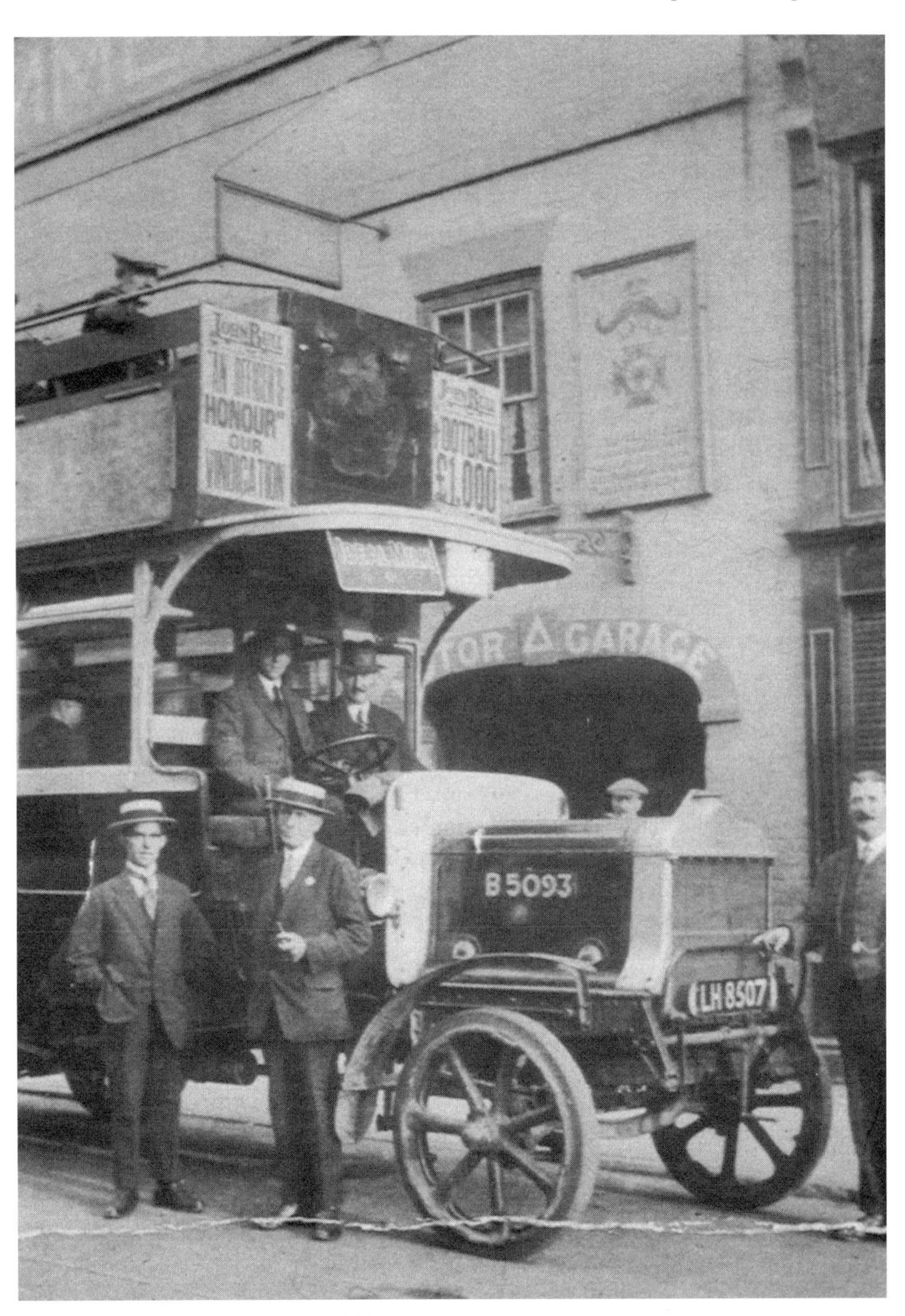

A National bus in Crouch Street around 1920. Pam Harris collection

and extreme patience was needed slowly to coax the unwilling engine into life. Even the passengers would sometimes be called upon to lend a hand when things got particularly tough, as recalled by former Colchester resident Joe Lawrence, who was born in 1903:

> I remember that the National had red buses in those days and they charged 6d ($2^1/_2$ p) to go to Halstead. I remember coming home from there on one occasion and having to get off and help to push the bus up the hill. We had to do that many a time.

Despite the fact that the old horse-drawn carrier carts were to be eventually superseded by the motor buses, many operators continued to carry parcels and run errands for people for a number of years to come. For example, on a typical run from Tollesbury to Colchester, the driver of an Osborne's bus might be given anything between twenty to thirty parcels to deliver, or errands to run during the day. Those operating on the Mersea or Brightlingsea routes would often be expected to carry boxes of live eels, and perhaps a box or two of winkles or oysters on the running boards.

Les Crick, who worked as a conductor for the Eastern National Omnibus Company in the 1930s, recalled that charges for carrying such items ranged from about 4d for a 7lb package and then graduated up to the higher amounts. He remembered that carrying and delivering parcels was a regular feature of the job at the time:

> I remember that a man from Great Horkesley use to have parcels of fish sent to him on regular occasions. They would be brought into the office, be stamped, the conductor would then sign for it and take it on his delivery sheet. Or you might be driving along some country road and see somebody standing at the bus stop with a big sack of spuds in front of them. When you pulled up they would put the sack on the bus, pay the delivery charge, and then be on their way, leaving us to manhandle this heavy sack and deliver it to the office at the other end.

The Day Colchester got its Ticket to Ride

It was a day long-awaited by the people of Colchester. On Thursday 28 July 1904, the town's tramway system was finally opened to the public. It was a terrible day weather-wise but that didn't stop hundreds of people lining the High Street, most with their umbrellas raised, to cheer on the Mayoress, Gertrude Barritt, as she powered up the first tramcar (No 13) and helped to drive it on its maiden journey to Lexden. In fact, the town had been waiting for this event to take place for more than twenty years following an aborted attempt in the 1880s to establish a steam-driven tramway. But now, by utilising new technology in the form of electricity, the town could finally boast the most modern of systems. In practical terms it meant that for the first time ever, cheap transport was made available for the masses.

The formal opening of Colchester's tramway system in July 1904. Author's collection

Fares averaged out at just a penny a mile, which was in stark contrast to the existing horse cab rates which could cost anything between 6d and a shilling to cover the same distance.

By the end of that first day alone (after just six hours of operation) the trams had carried more than 10,000 passengers, collecting over £42 in fares. And within just one hour of the opening ceremony having taken place, local photographer, William Gill, was offering souvenir picture postcards of the event for sale to the public. Among the thousands of people who flocked to have a ride on the new trams on that inaugural occasion was nine-year-old Harry Salmon who attended with his father:

> I remember my father taking me for a ride on the first trams when they opened in 1904. That was when they first started in Colchester and it was a very exciting ride on my part, but it was crowded with people wanting to ride on the trams. They thought it was wonderful, and from there on, of course, everyone used to ride the trams as there was no other form of mobility.

The initial fleet consisted of sixteen tramcars operating on routes to Lexden, North Station, East Gates and The Hythe, and in 1906 two additional trams were added on a route to the Recreation Ground. The contract for laying the tramlines and for fixing the overhead power cables had been awarded to the London firm of J G White & Co, and preliminary work, prior to track laying, had begun in October 1903 with the widening of North Bridge and other road improvements in Queen Street. The tracks, which were manufactured in Belgium, began arriving at The Hythe in January 1904. They each measured sixty feet in length and required the use of a huge trolley drawn by a traction engine to convey them to their final destination. Problems occurred almost immediately as the first batch of rails were being taken across town to Lexden. As the trolley was negotiating the awkward bend at the corner of St Botolph's Street and Magdalen Street, it mounted the pavement resulting in several of the tracks falling off and casing mayhem for some considerable time as workmen armed with jacks and other tackle struggled to put everything back into place.

The tracks were laid on a thick bed of concrete with the surrounding area paved with blocks of granite. In total the system comprised more than five miles of track and eleven miles of overhead cabling. The tracks were laid in both single and double sections with various passing places incorporated along the single runs. And in order to keep the overhead work as neat and as pleasing to the eye as possible, the cables and their support poles were all positioned on the right side of the road, whenever possible, when coming from North Station. The entire project took over six months to complete providing work for some 200 labourers.

The tramcars were built by the British Wagon & Carriage Co of Preston and supplied by the their associates Dick, Kerr & Co. They were all open-top double deckers

Tramcar No 11 climbing the steep gradient of North Hill. Author's collection

with room for forty-eight passengers (twenty-two inside and twenty-six outside), and were each fitted with two 35 hp engines designed to cope with the steep gradient of North Hill. They were constructed of mahogany, ash and maple with their exteriors finished in tuscan red and cream. The total cost of the entire operation, including the purchase of the initial sixteen trams, amounted to £55,000.

Tramcar No 13 driven by the Mayor and Mayoress arriving at Lexden terminus loaded with local dignitaries. Author's collection

The trams began their daily service at six in the morning and continued throughout the day, at fifteen minute intervals, until 11.30 at night. Both drivers and conductors were required to work a sixty-hour week, with wages ranging from 18s to 22s a week. Discipline was strictly maintained and those committing a serious offence such as speeding or failing to halt at a compulsory stop, faced immediate suspension or even dismissal. Harry Salmon (referred to earlier) went on to work as both a conductor and driver on the Colchester trams in the years leading up to the First World War, and was able to recall some of the conditions that he and the other conductors and drivers had to work under:

> Rules were very strict you know. You dare not miss a passenger if he was up the road somewhere, or you'd be for it. I can remember one day, when working as a conductor, being called into the office by the Chief Clerk, who asked me if I would be interested in learning how to become a driver and, of course, I jumped at the chance. Anyway, I had my time of instruction on the road under the supervision of a motorman (driver), and then I went into the sheds for a certain amount of time learning about the workings of a tram, before finally having to complete an oral examination before the General Manager. I can clearly remember that he asked me twelve questions and on the last question he said to me, 'You are going along Lexden Road with your tram at 2½ miles an hour and if a little child ran right across in front of your tram, what would you do?' 'Reverse and give the car power, Sir, I said. 'Have you not been taught never to use your magnetic brake like that?' he said to me. 'But you told me that I was only travelling at 2½ miles an hour and at that speed the motors wouldn't generate enough electricity to work the brakes', I said. 'Stop, get out of my office and don't think you know everything,' he said and with that I became a driver.

For those old enough to remember riding on the trams, the experience is one not easily forgotten. They were extremely noisy and as one respondent once claimed, 'they could be heard going up East Hill from as far away as Crockleford on a quiet day.' And although they travelled far quicker than one could possibly walk, they rarely reached speeds in excess of between 15-20 mph. In fact, this was probably due to the large number of stopping places along the various routes (there were five stopping places in the High Street alone) which required the tram to keep slowing down. In fact, one of the only flat stretches of track where the drivers could get some speed on occasions was along various sections of Lexden Road.

From the driver's point of view the most difficult part of the system to negotiate was the steep decline of North Hill. Harry Salmon recalled that the problem was particularly bad during wet weather:

> The trams that we drove weighed ten tons each and the most dangerous part of the job was going down North Hill. They were so heavy that you sometimes had difficulty stopping them. As soon as you gained sufficient speed you released your hand brake and pulled back your magnetic brake. It was the only way you could stop the tram, especially if it was a greasy morning – we would be pumping sand (on to the rails via a foot pedal) all the time in order to keep a grip on the rails. I can remember going down Hythe Hill one morning, the first tram down, and I very nearly ran right off the rails. I was pumping sand like the dickens and I only just stopped, the rails were so greasy.

Molly Schuessele (born 1914) had fond memories of riding on the trams:

> I used to ride on the trams many times. When we lived in Greenstead Road and I first went to the High School, mother used to give me the tram fare up the hill – of course, if I walked I could spend the 1d or 2d on myself. They were very rattlebang and made lots of noise. They had hard wooden seats with a slatted back which you could push either way so you could always face forward, which ever way the tram was going. The driver stood on a little platform, half moon shaped, with a handle, and a cord which operated a bell. The conductor had a band across his chest with a clip thing on it and a bag for the money. He would put your ticket into a machine before pressing a button which would put a hole in it. Where the hole was located would show where you had to get off the tram. The trams were all open top and rounded at the front and back, and the stairs went up in a part spiral. You had to hold on tight because they started off with a jerk. On the upper decks they had mackintoshes or tarpaulin covers across the seats with press studs which you could pull over your lap if it rained. The tramlines were in the middle of the road so when the tram stopped and you wanted to get off, you had to make sure that nothing was coming before you crossed the road to get to the kerb.

Tramlines being removed in Crouch Street in the 1950s. Author's collection

This redundant tramcar was converted into a road side café at Langenhoe. Colchester Museums

Tramcar No 10, Colchester's last surviving tram, in its former resting place, as a garden shed at Great Horkesley. Roger Harvey

Despite the obvious convenience of the trams, the network itself was extremely limited and, increasing competition from outside motor bus companies, particularly during the 1920s, finally led the council to abandon the service in 1929 in favour of a fleet of new motor buses. The overhead wiring was taken down but the most of the poles, which had held the cabling remained in place for several years acting as lamp standards. Most of the rails were simply covered over and were finally removed during the 1940s and 1950s. A few sections, however, still remain and in the former tramway shed in Magdalen Street, which is now used as the bus depot, a number of sixty foot lengths of track still exist alongside the vehicle service pits.

But what became of the old trams after they were taken out of service? We know that several were sold to local building firm Moss & Co for use as site huts at £5 each. Another was converted into a roadside café at Langenhoe and several others were

An advertising window panel from tramcar No 10. Roger Harvey

converted into garden sheds, including one which used to stand in a prominent position in Harwich Road. Despite reports in recent times that one of these old trams was to make a spectacular comeback nothing has ever materialised – at least that is until now. For against all the odds we can now report that at least one old Colchester tram, in part at least, has survived and may yet live to see another day.

The tram in question is No 10 of the original fleet of 18 and for more than sixty years languished in a garden at Great Horkesley where the lower deck of the vehicle had been converted into a garden shed and given a tin roof (an act which probably saved it from decay). In 1996, the tram was removed to a secure location in another part of the county and is currently being restored by a local tram enthusiast. At the time of writing much of the original framework and fittings have been stripped down while it is being repaired and cleaned up. The plan is for the tram to be fully restored to working order and put on display on a special trackway which is also being prepared.

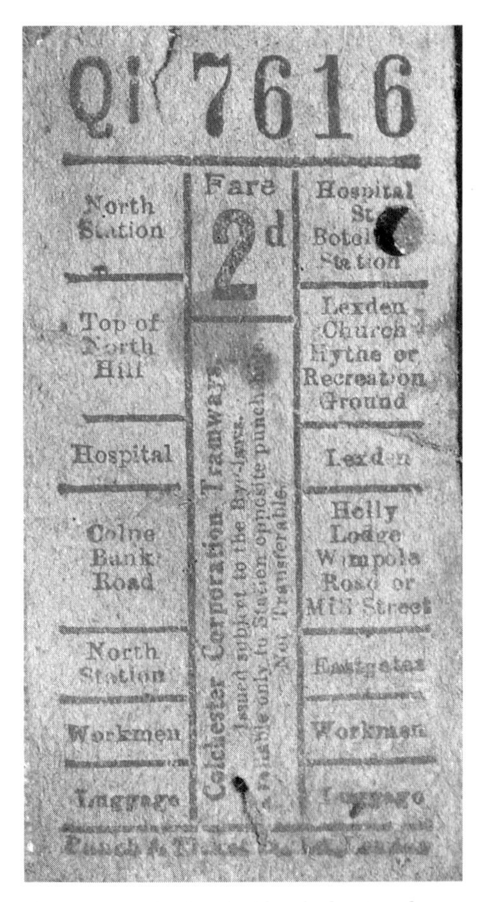

A used tram ticket found within the framing of tram-car No 10 during restoration work. The Author

CHAPTER 6

TRADE AND INDUSTRY

Final Port of Call for the Hythe

Colchester's historic medieval port was finally closed in 2001, bringing to an end a centre of local activity stretching back over 800 years. Exactly when the harbour was first built is not known, but early records would suggest a date of around 1200, or even earlier. Despite its great age, however, it was not the first harbour or port in the town, a fact suggested by its very title the 'New Hythe' in medieval records. This, of course, would indicate the existence of an earlier harbour or 'Old Hythe' predating the present site.

In fact, a harbour, or at least some kind of landing stage for sea-going vessels, is thought to have existed in Colchester as far back as the late Iron Age in the area known today as

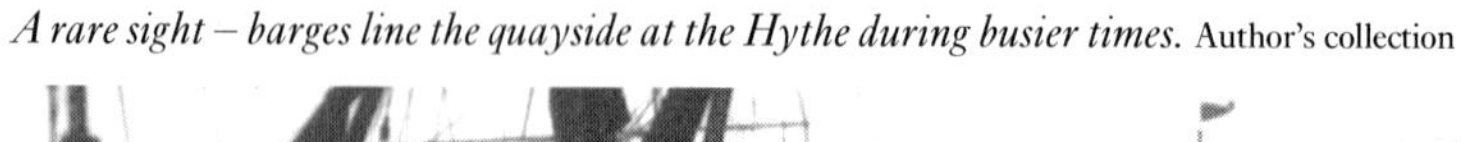

A rare sight – barges line the quayside at the Hythe during busier times. Author's collection

Sheepen, close to the present-day St Helena School. Archaeological excavations carried out during the 1930s uncovered a whole range of pre-Roman finds from what would appear to have been some kind of industrial complex which would probably have been served by a port or landing area for vessels sailing up the Colne river.

With the coming of the Romans in AD 43, trade between Britain and the Continent would have intensified and provisions for receiving and unloading sea-going vessels close to the new fortress, and later the new town, would have been established. Precisely where this Roman harbour was located, however, is not known, but quarrying work concentrated near Fingringhoe in the 1930s unearthed numerous Roman finds which may suggest some kind of port, or military supply base being built at this point on the river. From hereon, smaller vessels could then have travelled further upstream to a smaller landing area nearer to the fortress or town, possibly somewhere near the present harbour, or at a point further upstream near the Castle Park. The idea that the Roman harbour may have been close to the present site is based on the fact that at least two Roman roads are thought to converge on the area, but this may account for nothing more than the site having been a convenient crossing place on the river.

Despite not knowing the exact location of the Roman harbour, we do know that following the end of the Roman period, and the coming of the Saxons, a new harbour was established further downstream alongside what is known as the 'old channel' close to present-day Old Heath. In fact, the name 'Old Heath' would appear to have derived from 'Old Hythe', a

In this view of the quayside a barge is being loaded with hay bound for the London market. When fully loaded these barges looked very much like floating haystacks and were known as 'Stackies'. Author's collection

name which stems from the Saxon 'Hetha' signifying a harbour. The old channel was located on what is now mainly marsh land lying between Colchester and Rowhedge and was learly still identifiable as such on late nineteenth century maps. The historian Philip Morant, when writing in the eighteenth century, was able to claim that the Old Hythe was so named because 'wares and merchandises brought to this town by water used to be unloaded there.' And though he was of the opinion that the old harbour must have been out of use for some 500 years, he recited a case, just 100 years earlier (c.1650), where a witness had sworn that he had passed by a small boat up the channel or creek where ships, anciently, went up to the Old Hythe.

With the coming of the Normans it must have been decided that a more convenient harbour closer to the town was required, and the old site was eventually abandoned. The earliest references to this new harbour are found in documents dating from the 1220s, although the site had probably been in use several years earlier. As noted above, the new harbour became known as the New Hythe, a term which survived until well into the seventeenth century. What is perhaps more interesting is the fact that the term Old Hythe was still being used in connection with Old Heath as late as the early 1900s.

The new harbour prospered throughout the Middle Ages, becoming the economic centre of the town – coal, grain, cloth, fish and timber being just some of the regular cargoes handled at the port. At the time of the Siege of Colchester in 1648, we learn that the besieged Royalist army was able to procure from the port large quantities of 'corn and wine of all sorts, with much salt, some fish and a great quantity of powder'. A drawing of the town in the eighteenth century shows The Hythe as a bustling centre of activity with numerous sailing vessels and warehousing lining the quay.

But is was probably during the nineteenth century, at a time when Colchester experienced its own version of the Industrial Revolution, that the port entered into what has become known as its 'heyday', or more prosperous years which, despite one or two periods of slump or recession, continued right through to the middle years of the twentieth century. Between the years 1860–1900, some two or three thousand ships were using the port each year, carrying between them more than a million tons of cargo. The port at this time was a hive of activity with a whole range of industrial outlets lining the quayside, including coal and timber yards, gasworks, an oil mill, grain merchants and maltings.

The area also acted as a magnet for generations of children who would wile away their leisure hours exploring every nook and cranny along the quayside. A favourite stopping place was outside Parry's oil mill where, through open doors, one could stand entranced as linseed oil poured out of the large presses.

Bill Warner (1910–2000) had fond memories of this and recounted the following experience:

> You could stand down at Parry's when the doors were open and see the old presses pressing the linseed into cattle cake, and see the oil pouring out. They used to press it into cake and it was hard as a rock, but when

> the linseed oil had come out, it was pumped up into the tanks and measured off into the barrels.

Charles Herbert (1896–1992) recalled trips to the gas works to fetch back barrels of coke:

> My father used to know a man who worked down at the gas works on the furnace. And we used to take a barrow down there and he would fill it up with coke, as well as a big bag full on top, then he would put it on the scales and weigh it and we'd bring it away. We paid about a shilling (5p) for it.

Bill Warner who had wonderful memories of the old port area. The Author

Other activities recalled were perhaps a little more dangerous. Alice Farthing (born 1908) lived as a child in Hythe Station Road, next to the *Sun Inn*, and remembered happy days playing on the riverbank:

> When we were young, during the war, several of us girls used to go down the ladder in the river and pull all the old iron out, clean it and drag it up to Wheeler's scrap yard in an old pram. He would give us a few coppers for it. One day when we were down in the river we had to come up because the tide was coming in, and as we were coming up the ladder a policeman got hold of us and gave us a good hiding. He then said, 'Now you go home and your mothers will give you another one.' We were crying and he gave us a good talking to and said that he never wanted to see us in the river again – but we never took any notice – we went down again the next day.

For most people, however, one of the most endearing memories of The Hythe and its industry, is the sight of the old Thames sailing barges winding their way up the river to one of the moorings along the quay, or up as far East Mill. Frank Thompson (born 1921), who lives at Layer-de-la-Haye, used to work on the barges and remembers some of the difficulties encountered in trying to negotiate the series of low bridges on the final run up to the Mill:

Frank Thompson, 2005

First of all you had to lower your mast and gear flat down onto the deck. Then as soon as you were afloat you had to push the barge up the river with booms – long poles about twenty-five feet long – you'd put them in the water, or on the bank, set it against your shoulder, and you walked the length of the barge. When you got to the end of the barge you'd pull it up and walk back again. The first bridge we had to go under was Hythe bridge, and then you'd got the two railway bridges, and then the road bridge by the Mill. From Hythe bridge it would take about an hour and a half to push our way up to the Mill – which is about a mile. Once we got to the Mill we would have to heave our mast and gear back up so that they could get to the hold to unload. I've seen

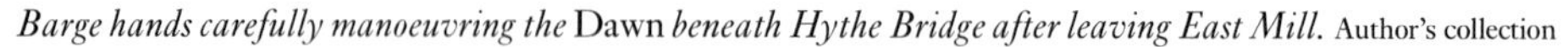

Barge hands carefully manoeuvring the Dawn *beneath Hythe Bridge after leaving East Mill.* Author's collection

as many as four or five barges up there at once all queuing to be unloaded, which could take a couple of days, or longer, depending on where you were in the queue.

The final decline of the port has been rapid. Even as late as the mid 1970s, some 2,000 vessels were still visiting the port each year carrying more than 600,000 tons of cargo. And yet within twenty years this number had dwindled to less than 200. Today the trade has diminished altogether. Coupled with losses amounting to tens of thousands of pounds annually, a good thing inevitably had to come to an end. But what of the future? Ambitious plans have been put forward to revitalise the whole area which may include the building of yet another new harbour, or waterside village with marina and other leisure facilities. Only time will tell, but one wonders what historians will be writing about the place in another 800 years time!

The end of an era – one of the last ships to leave the port. The Author

Directory Success

Reports of redundancies and factory closures are forever making headline news. Words such as 'downsizing' and 'outsourcing' are fast becoming part of our standard vocabulary, and so when we do occasionally hear of a company that appears to be bucking the trend and actually expanding their activities, it is encouraging to take a closer look. One such company is bgp of Colchester (formerly Benham and Co Ltd) who in the last few years have embarked upon an ambitious programme of expansion at their Severalls Lane factory. The firm specialises in the production of telephone directories and various other directory-type publications and are currently enjoying perhaps their best years ever. The company has been part of the town's history for more than 150 years, and in the following study we look at some of the men and women who have played a part in the firm's success – but be warned, the story is a little complicated!

Edward Benham founder of the Colchester printing firm. BGP

It all began with a small advertisement posted in a local newspaper in January 1846, which read: 'Thomas Knibb, Bookseller, Stationer, Bookbinder, Music & Print Seller at 15 High Street, Colchester announces his retirement and Edward Benham has taken over the business.' This brief announcement heralded the beginning of what was to become the well known publishing company Benham and Co Ltd. Edward and his wife Mary set up their home above the shop and were later joined in their endeavours by their sons William Gurney (known as Gurney) and Charles.

By 1852 Edward had sold off the bookselling side of the firm to W H Smith and had set himself up as a general printer. In 1867, along with business partners Henry Harrison and Thomas Ralling, he took over the *Essex Standard* newspaper and moved the operation to new premises at 19 High Street. The newspaper had been established in 1831 by the Reverend George Tufnell as a mechanism to further his political conservative interests. Tufnell later sold the paper to John Taylor, who remained its owner and editor until 1866. Edward's personal interest in the venture, however, was to be short lived, for he died of consumption just two years later in 1869, at the age of forty-seven. By this time, Thomas Ralling had already relinquished his interest in the firm, leaving Edward's widow Mary to become joint-owner with the remaining partner Henry Harrison.

W Gurney Benham – tireless worker and former editor of Benham & Co Ltd. BGP

When Harrison himself retired in 1879, Mary became sole proprietor before being joined in the business by her two sons Gurney and Charles. Gurney became editor in 1884 and continued in the role until 1943. During all of this time, over fifty-nine years, and despite being involved in numerous other social and public activities, he continued to write his weekly column 'Colchester County Notes' without let up, fifty-two weeks of the year. He was indeed a remarkable man. He was elected to the Town Council in 1892, served as Mayor of Colchester on three occasions, and played a leading role in the building of the new town hall and public library. One of his greatest literary achievements was the publication of his monumental *Benham's Book of Quotations* which sold to a worldwide audience over a forty year period. The final edition of the book contained more than 50,000 literary quotations. In the 1880s he published the first *Colchester Directory* and by the late 1890s was publishing a local street directory full of names and addresses of the town's inhabitants on an annual basis. He was also a keen historian and found time to translate several volumes of old borough records from their medieval Latin. Perhaps his greatest accolade, however, was the receiving of his knighthood in 1935, and being elected an Honorary Freeman and High Steward of his home town of Colchester. Following his death in 1944, at the age of eighty-five, his son Hervey, who was to inherit the business, wrote of his late father, 'How was such a mass of activity crowded into one lifetime?'

After Sir Gurney's death the running of the business, as noted above, was taken over by his son Hervey who remained at the helm of things until his own retirement nearly forty years later. He once recalled his first impression of the High Street printing works back in the late 1920s. 'I was horrified,' he said. 'Although there were a couple of monotype keyboards in the composition room, much of the setting was still being done by hand by a row of eight girls on piecework, all perched upon a long stool consisting of a bit of board nailed to the top of a piece of two by two, with a wad of dirty newspapers for a cushion.'

At this time the activities of the business were split fairly equally between the work of jobbing printing and newspaper publishing. But things were soon to change, and particularly with the appointment of Tom Hart in 1945. Tom was from a family of Northamptonshire printers and was soon to become joint managing director with Hervey Benham. From here on there followed a gradual separation of the ways. The newspaper side of things developed its own printing resources and moved to new premises at the rear of the High Street office, and the printing side of things was later sold to the Hutchingson Publishing Group, who under the direction of Tom Hart (who had retained the title 'Benham and Co Ltd') relocated to a new site in Sheepen Road. And it is this branch of the business, of course, that is the main focus of this study.

Things were also changing back on the newspaper side of things which had now become known as 'Benham's Newspapers Ltd'. In 1952, Hervey Benham joined forces with Arnold Quick (a newspaper publisher and printer from Clacton) to form QB Printers Limited (Quick and Benham). The new partnership prospered and good profits were made by printing other people's papers on contract, in addition to their own local editions. They too later relocated their printing works to the Sheepen Road site, right next door to the printing works of Benham and Co Ltd managed by Tom Hart. In 1970, the Colchester and Clacton series of newspapers were merged to form Essex County Newspapers Ltd, and in the early 1980s the entire operation was sold to Reed International. At this point Hervey Benham finally bowed out of the business, bringing to an end his family's long direct association in the local printing and newspaper industry.

Female compositors at the Culver Street works in the 1930s. BGP

Hervey Benham, second from left – grandson of the founder and the last in the family line to run the business. BGP

Meanwhile, in 1973, the fortunes of Benham and Co Ltd (the printing side) took another step forward with the sale of the company to the McCorquodale Group, who transformed the Sheepen Road site into the main production centre for Lloyds of London Press when it moved its headquarters to Colchester the following year. Part of the deal included a fifteen year contract for Benham's to print the Lloyds List, a useful contract which was to pave the way to even greater prosperity during the 1970s and 1980s. In the early 1990s yet another programme of expansion resulted in the firm moving to a new factory complex on the Severalls Industrial Estate on the outskirts of Colchester.

By this time the contract to print the Lloyds List had diminished somewhat and the company had been sold to yet new owners. There had also been a concerted effort in the late 1980s to diversify their activities away from the printing of newspapers into more specialised publications such as motoring and property journals and directories. And it was this latter activity that was to emerge as the dominant feature of the company's modern-day activities. The turning point came in 1997 when the company was purchased by the Goodhead Group and subsequently secured a lucrative contract with BT to print all the UK telephone directories. In statistical terms, this relates to around twenty-five million copies a year, with Colchester receiving 210,000 and Ipswich 146,000 of that number. In

Modern day compositors – Tony Petter (left) and Viv Marsh prepare an electronic version of a BT telephone book ready for plate-making. EADT

order to be competitive in this highly specialist field, the company has had to embark upon an ambitious £20 million pound programme of expansion which resulted in the installation of a new highly technical printing machine and bindery unit. The bindery unit, which is capable of binding up to 15,000 directories per hour, is housed in a new factory unit which has almost doubled the size of the existing production space.

Paul Taylor, Operations Manager for the Colchester end of the business, is rightly proud of the firm's achievements:

> Prospects are excellent. We are developing all the time and continuously looking to develop further into the directory and catalogue market. In addition to the telephone directory contract, we print holiday brochures, railway time tables – in fact, anything that looks like a directory. And in a typical year we will get through more than 30,000 tons of paper.

This is certainly good news for the 140 staff currently employed by the firm. The production line operates six days a week around the clock, with Saturday the only time that the presses are silent.

And finally to the new name 'bgp'. Well it stands for 'benhamgoodheadprint'. Goodhead Print and Benham and Co Ltd formerly merged in November 2001 and it was decided that because of the antiquity associated with the name Benham, that this should be reflected in the new trading name. Having made that decision it was also agreed that the name

This giant Lithoman web off-set press, one of the largest in Europe, is capable of producing up to 40,000 copies an hour. EADT

This carousel receives up to 15,000 directories an hour as they pass through the bindery unit before being trimmed.
EADT

Goodhead should also be included, so hence the new company name. At least the family name of Benham has survived into the twenty-first century. I wonder what Edward Benham, the founder of the firm, would have made of it all? I think he would have been impressed.

Postscript
Since the above article was first compiled in 2002, the business activities of BGP have suffered something of a setback. In January 2006, the firm announced that after failing to renew the lucrative BT telephone directory contract (BT had decided to move their production operations overseas), the company was facing closure. In March, however, the firm announced that a last minute rescue package had been put together with the aim of saving the company and the jobs of about half the workforce. One hopes that the firm will be able to fully turn things around in the near future and return to a period of successful trading.

A Blooming Good Business

If Isaac Bunting, the founder of the Bunting Nursery business on the outskirts of Colchester, had been alive today he may well have followed a similar career to that of well known television presenter Alan Titchmarsh. For way back in 1828, in a book that he published on the different species of plants, he was offering to visit clients in their own homes to give advice and instruction on horticulture and botany. Perhaps he could even be described as the first ever garden makeover expert!

William Bunting son of Isaac the founder. Prue James collection

Isaac was born in the Mile End district of Colchester in 1783, one of seven children born to William and Margaret Bunting. Little is known of his formative years but by the time he was seventeen he was working for various local farmers and other landowners as a day gardener and horticulturist. He married Elizabeth Franklin of St Martin's parish in 1807 and in 1819, at the age of thirty-six, set up in business as an independent nursery and seedsman in Lexden Road. The business prospered with early contracts including the setting out of the grounds of the new Essex County Hospital and maintenance of the same on an annual contract.

By the 1830s three of his sons, William, Isaac and Horatio had joined him in the Lexden Road business. Around this time Isaac Snr purchased an additional twenty acres of land in North Station Road. There he set up his eldest son William in a newly-built house, which later became known as the North Nursery. By this time Isaac was also being described in a local directory as a florist, suggesting the possible propagation of flowers under glass at this relatively early date.

When Isaac Snr died in 1850, the business was divided between his two surviving sons William and Horatio (Isaac the younger having died in 1846), with the former inheriting the North Nursery and Horatio the Lexden Road site. However, whilst William apparently prospered at the North Nursery, Horatio soon got himself into financial difficulties and in 1856 was declared bankrupt with debts of more than £2,000. He had apparently mortgaged the entire Lexden Road business and the bank was calling time on his borrowing. Horatio disappears from the record at this point leaving his brother William and a family friend to buy back the Lexden Road business from the creditors at considerable expense.

For the next forty years the business prospered under William's leadership. Contracts for the firm included the planting of the new cemetery in Mersea Road, the laying out of the gardens at the new seaside towns of Clacton and Walton and becoming the preferred contractor to the Borough Council providing floral decorations for numerous civic functions including the annual Oyster Feast.

By the 1870s, William's three sons, William Ellis, Alfred and Isaac had joined the family firm and were all working hard to make the business a success. But it was his youngest son Isaac, born in 1850, whose entrepreneurial activities were to have a profound influence on

A Bunting family group photograph from 1877. Prue James collection

the future success of the firm. For in 1877, Isaac withdrew his total savings of £22 from his parental run savings account, and made the long journey to Yokohama in Japan where he set himself up as a lily bulb exporter. By any standards, this was a monumental achievement. After enduring a long and potentially hazardous sea passage and having little or no knowledge of the customs of language of his new home, he was within a few months of leaving his native shores, exporting Japanese lily bulbs back to England by the boat load. His father, William, and two brothers back in England were adapting the home business to cope with the phenomenal demand for this new commodity, which was to eventually account for a major part of the firm's turnover in the years to come.

By all accounts, Isaac was a canny individual demanding cash payment up front in Japan before releasing the bulbs on their perilous journey back to England. This is seen from the contents of one of his first trade catalogues printed in Yokohama in 1885 which states that 'I require cash at Yokohama as soon as the goods are safely packed and on board the mail boats. Once on board all goods are forwarded at the owner's risk, but insurance can be affected if desired against total loss or damage by salt water.'

Alfred Bunting from North Nursery. Author's collection

Isaac Bunting, the young entrepreneur who set up his own branch of the family business in Japan. Prue James collection

Isaac regularly made the long journey back to England bringing gifts and Japanese novelties for his family and friends. On one such journey home he married a local girl named Ann French before returning to Japan to raise a family. By the early 1900s, the opening of the new Trans-Siberian Railway between Moscow and Vladivostock would have made the journey to Japan somewhat easier, although still requiring an overland journey of some 6,000 miles and a 400 mile sea crossing.

The Japanese side of the business continued to thrive until after the First World War when the wild lily bulbs started becoming scarce. By this time, however, the bulbs were beginning to be successfully cultivated back home in England, and it would appear that around this time Isaac retired to Vancouver in Canada where he continued in the lily bulb business until his death in the 1920s.

Back home in England Isaac's father William had died in 1895 and left the Lexden Road business to his eldest son William Ellis, and the North Nursery in trust to provide an income for his two unmarried daughters Harriet and Julia. Alfred, the remaining son, was left with just a small piece of land near the barracks which he subsequently sold, and after renting land from his two sisters set up on his own account at the North Nursery.

A division in the family firm occurred at this point with a distinct separating of the ways between William Ellis and his son William Whorlow, who had retained the original trading name 'Bunting and Sons' at the Lexden Road site, and Alfred who was working on his own account at the North Nursery. For the next few years it was the Lexden Road branch of the family business that was to gain some prominence in securing a number of important local contracts. William Whorlow, in particular, became quite active in local affairs and is still remembered as the benefactor of the Bunting Rooms, a gymnasium for the youth of the town.

In 1916, after the death of William Ellis, the Lexden Road site descended to William Whorlow who continued to run the business until his own death in 1922. At this time an even deeper rift occurred between the two branches of the family when it was discovered that William Whorlow, who had married, but remained childless, had left the entire Lexden Road business to one of his workers at the expense of either his uncle Alfred or several cousins. As it turned out, William Whorlow must have greatly over estimated the worth and business acumen of this particular employee for within a few years the business had failed and the land was sold off.

Fortunately, at this time, Eric Bunting, son of Alfred, was able to buy back the family trading name of 'Bunting and Sons' for the use of the North Nursery side of the business. Following his father Alfred's death in 1926, Eric took charge of affairs and was instrumental in guiding the firm to its present day success. He was ably assisted by his son Peter and subsequently his grandsons Stephen and Benjamin, and by this time the strength of the business had shifted significantly from the sale of lily bulbs towards the propagation of tomato plants. In the 1970s, the firm sold off the North Nursery site for building development and relocated the business to Great Horkesley on the outskirts of Colchester.

William Ellis (seated) and wife Polly with sons George (left) and William Whorlow. Prue James collection

And so on to the present day – and finally what appears to be the sad end of the Bunting Nursery business. Increased competition from abroad has made it increasingly difficult to make ends meet in a strong competitive market. But while this may signal the end of the nursery side of the business after a run of nearly 200 years, ambitious plans are still being considered to redevelop the site into a special John Constable Heritage Centre. In addition to the historical aspects of the venture, the new-look site would incorporate a number of rural craft outlets, a restaurant and garden centre. Initial plans, however, have met with some opposition from local people who feel that the increased number of visitors and

The former office building at North Nursery. Author's collection

traffic the venture would generate would be too much for the area to cope with. So, for the time being, it is back to the drawing board in an attempt to come up with an acceptable compromise that will allow the venture to proceed and hopefully inject a new lease of life into this old family firm. I for one support the initiative and believe that Isaac the originator of the family business would have as well.

CHAPTER 7

VILLAGE LIFE

A Farming Community with a Rich History

The rising interest in family and community history has prompted many village communities to set up their own local history societies, or smaller groups of enthusiasts to research and record their own little corner of this fair land. In the main their activities include investigating and recording old buildings, collecting and preserving old photographs and recording the memories of local residents. Many have also gone as far as publishing some of their findings in the form of short histories, or compilations of old photographs. It was in connection with this latter activity that resulted in my paying a visit to Fingringhoe, a small village on the outskirts of Colchester, where in 1998 the local Historical Recorders Group published a delightful collection of old photographs of the area entitled *Fingringhoe: Past and Present*.

Thatched cottages on Church Green, c.1905. Fingringhoe Historical Recorders Group

The village is located about two miles to the south-east of Colchester and lies along a low ridge of land which runs in a westerly direction from the River Colne. To the north- east, and looking back towards Colchester, there are picturesque views of the Roman River Valley with its patchwork quilt of green fields and hedgerows, whilst in the opposite direction the land gradually descends to the River Colne and a large area of salt marsh which is home to a wide variety of birds.

As far as the historic shape of the village is concerned it is difficult to pinpoint where things all began as the community seems to have developed, in piecemeal fashion, over a fairly wide area, resulting in numerous pockets of housing dotted around the parish. For example, in previous years the village is known to have had at least three greens, each supporting its own mini community, although the original heart of the village must surely have been centred on the area known as Church Green, where one will find the village church, the local pub and the village school.

It is likely that a community of sorts has existed here since Roman times. During gravel extraction work at Fingringhoe Wick (the site of the present day nature reserve) in the1920s and 1930s, the remains of at least two Roman villas were discovered as well as evidence of some form of military encampment dating from the Claudian period. It is thought that this may have been used as a supply base for the legionary fortress in Colchester and a place where goods brought up river by larger vessels could have been transferred to smaller craft to complete their journey up river. And following the passing of the Roman period, it is likely that some continuity of settlement went on through to the Saxon period as the village name itself appears to have Saxon origins, possibly signifying a finger of land upon a ridge, or a hill.

Although the village, or manor of Fingringhoe, is not mentioned by name in the *Domesday Book* of 1086, it is referred to in an eleventh century charter of Edward the Confessor when it was included in a grant made of West Mersea to the Abbey of St Ouen at Rouen in Normandy. Throughout much of the Middle Ages the Fingringhoe manor remained tied to West Mersea, under French ownership, before returning to the English Crown at the time of the suppression of alien priories in the reign of Henry V. In 1422 the manors of Mersea, Fingringhoe and Pete Hall were granted to the Archbishop of Canterbury where they remained until the time of the Dissolution. From here on the estate passed into private ownership and descended through various families until recent times.

Despite the upheavals of the Reformation – and the granting of the Fingringhoe and Mersea estates into private ownership – the manor court, where all affairs of the manor were managed and regulated, continued as before. Local customs and dues affecting both the lord and his tenants continued to be rigidly enforced. For example, according to a surviving custumal of the Manors of West Mersea and Fingringhoe, whenever a copyhold tenant died the lord was entitled to claim the best beast from his estate as a kind of death duty tax: 'The lorde shall have his best beaste whatsoever it be, horse, oxe, cowe, shepe, swyne, pyge, goose, cocke, or henn' For the lord's part, he too had certain duties and

St Andrew's Church, Fingringhoe. Fingringhoe Historical Recorders Group

arrangements to perform on behalf of his tenants, including maintaining a bull or a boar for their use: 'Also that the lorde or his fermor (farmer) at euery of these townes of Westmersey and Fingregoe doe yerely kepe a comon bull and a boore for the easement of the tenantes.'

At the time of the 1801 census the population of the village was 464, representing perhaps up to a hundred families scattered among the 3,000 acres of farm and marsh land. The country at this time was still embroiled in the first of the Napoleonic Wars and when peace was declared in October of that year most of the villagers went on a four day-long 'bender'. A diary of the period kept by local farmer, Joseph Page, describes in some detail what took place:

> Oct. 14, 1801: This day much rejoicing took place here on account of a peace being made between Great Britain and the French Republic. The morning was ushered in by ringing of bells and the firing of canon, and the tops of houses and other conspicuous places were decorated by flags and various devices. Two large booths were erected on the green, and to add to the general festivity a bullock was roasted whole, filled with potatoes, and a great deal of beer and other liquors was given to the populace. It was supposed that the number of people of all descriptions assembled was not less than fifteen hundred, and upwards of seventy pounds of gunpowder was fired away, with an abundance of fireworks of different sorts.

On the following day a large number of villagers, many still tipsy from the night before, marched through the village, carrying flags and dragging a cannon, before arriving at the

The Whalebone *public house in 2004.* The Author

Whalebone public house where they sang *God Save the King* and other songs of victory. Farmer Page records that the celebrations continued in a similar vein for several more days before grinding to a halt on the night of 17 October, by which time Mr John Cooper, of Fingringhoe Hall, had parted with more than £100 in helping to finance the celebrations.

The nineteenth century brought little in the way of change to the inhabitants of the village. Fingringhoe remained very much an agricultural community with most of the male population being engaged in farm work of some kind or another and earning perhaps ten or twelve shillings a week. At the time of the 1881 census, in addition to the large numbers of agricultural labourers working on the land, there were also three shepherds, two brickmakers, a thatcher, a blacksmith, a miller and two mole catchers!

Most of the inhabitants at this time would grow their own vegetables and many went as far as keeping a pig or two in their back gardens, often just a few feet away from their back door. There were no restrictions in those days as to how the pigs were kept, or indeed slaughtered, and many owners would compete with one another as to who could raise the heaviest pig in the shortest amount of time. When the animal had reached a certain size – usually about eight stone – it would be killed on the spot by a local butcher, or pig killer. The pig would be held on a stool with a noose around it nose, before its throat was cut and its blood allowed to drain into a pail. It would then be placed into a tub of scalding water and scraped until the skin was clean of bristles before being hung by its hind legs on a post and split down the middle. It would then be left for a day or so to cool down before being

A water carrier selling water door to door. Author's collection

removed and cut into joints. At this stage of the operation several local boys would have gathered to await their special prize – the pig's bladder which they would blow up and use as a football.

Home comforts such as running water or indoor sanitation were unheard of until well into the twentieth century, and most people got their water from one of three local springs. Most toilets consisted of nothing more than a small hut over a deep hole in the garden, which would have been emptied on a regular basis and the contents dug into the ground. In fact the water from the spring opposite the *Whalebone* public house was of a superior quality and was taken by horse and cart to the neighbouring villages of Abberton and Langenhoe where it was sold to householders for a penny a pail.

Although most modern day residents of Fingringhoe are able to enjoy all the comforts of modern life, there are still a few older residents who are able to look back with some fondness to the Fingringhoe of old. One such person is eighty-one-year-old Joan Beales who has been a resident of the village since the early 1930s and has happy memories of leaving school and starting work at Fingringhoe Hall (the old manor house):

> I had to start work at 6.30 in the morning and we were still more or less on duty until we went to bed at about 10 'clock at night. Our first job in the morning was

making porridge for all the staff before making toast for the family. I would then have to run a bath for Mrs Furneaux before making a start on the housework. In the afternoons I would often take the dogs for a walk, which I enjoyed because I was out in the open air. I had two uniforms – a pink and white check one for the mornings, and a blue and white one for the afternoons. There were several staff working there including a housemaid, a cook, a pantry boy and a butler, and we all slept up in the attic part of the building.

Greta Buy can also remember life in the village back in the 1930s and 1940s – recalling the days when tradesmen made weekly visits to the village selling all kinds of groceries and other produce:

Our milk was delivered by Percy Hopkins who used to come round the village on a lady's bicycle. He would have two large churns hanging from each of his handlebars, and another one on a carrier at the back. We also had two bakers who used to call, and two oil vans (Charlie Brown's and the Co-op) who used to stock nearly everything bar the kitchen sink. When they used to call, you

Residents today: Daphne Allen, Greta Buy and Joan Beales. The Author

would give them your order for the following week, because we didn't have any telephones then. I can also remember when people wanted the doctor they would hang a piece of white cloth on the hedge or fence outside the houses to let him know him know that they wanted him to call. The ferry (to and from Wivenhoe) was also used by lots of people in the village. They used to bring milk and coal over the river from Wivenhoe and even the newspapers arrived by the ferry after being delivered to Wivenhoe railway station from Colchester.

Although much of the land around Fingringhoe is still being used for agricultural purposes, the days when the land provided work for large numbers of local farm workers is a thing of the past. But for one local resident those days are certainly not forgotten. Daphne Allen, a Fingringhoe resident for more than sixty years, was able to achieve her ambition of working on a farm when she left school at the age of sixteen:

All I ever wanted to do when I was a young girl was to work on a farm and so when I left school I managed to get a job at Fingringhoe Hall, which was then owned by Colonel and Mrs Furneaux. I remember that she was an excellent lady farmer who could turn her hand to any kind of farm work. I started at lambing time and quickly learnt how to milk a sheep when a lamb wouldn't suckle. I also learnt how to take a skin from a dead lamb and put it onto another lamb so that the mother ewe would think it was hers, and let it suckle. When the lambs' tails were docked I would take a bundle home to my mother who would skin them and make a sort of lambs' tail broth.

There was also a small herd of Friesian cows which we milked in the old cowshed. On cold mornings we would warm our hands in the lovely soft pouch between the cow's udder and their back leg. Some were very sweet tempered, but the bad tempered ones used to kick you and would sometimes send the pail of milk flying into the gutter. We had to cool the milk by lifting the heavy buckets of milk high above our heads and tipping the milk into the cooler, from where it ran down over a series of pipes which were full of cold running water. After milking there would always be a row of farm cats waiting to sample the milk, and I too used to like drinking the warm milk straight from the cow.

We also had two lovely Suffolk Punch horses named Punch and Blossom. I used to work these horses with harrows and a horse-rake and would have to walk behind, up and down, acre after acre. If the horses stopped suddenly for some reason you could get your feet entangled in the harrows – I'm sure that I must have nodded off at times whilst walking up and down. I also used to have to take the horses up to Mr Fookes, the blacksmith, to be shod. I hated the smell of burning hoof when he had made the red-hot shoe and was trying it out on the horse. I know the horse didn't feel anything, but I certainly did!

One of Essex's Finest Treasures

Which village has been described as the 'most attractive small town in Essex' and was made famous by the artist John Constable? The answer, of course, is Dedham, a community of some 2,000 inhabitants lying by the River Stour on the Suffolk border. Even today, Dedham retains many of the features that so appealed to John Constable and which, on one occasion, prompted him to say to his wife: 'I wish we had a little house here.' The place is full of charm and wonderful old buildings, not least the splendid Perpendicular church of St Mary the Virgin which dominates the main street. In fact, the internationally renowned architectural historian Nikolaus Pevsner made the comment that 'there is nothing at Dedham to hurt the eye.'

Our short exploration of the village then, will begin with the church, which was built between 1492 (the year that Columbus 'discovered America') and 1520. It was built in the Perpendicular style and is perhaps more akin to the famous Suffolk churches of the period rather than those of Essex. Its massive tower stands 131 feet high and incorporates an unusual passageway running through its base which would have provided access around the building without the need for leaving consecrated ground. The church, like many others of the style in East Anglia, was built at a time when the cloth trade was at its peak and when many local clothiers were becoming very wealthy. Indeed, they were the 'multi-millionaires' of their time and their wealth was reflected in the churches which they helped to build.

Dedham church. EADT

One of the more interesting aspects of the church's history, and indeed that of Dedham as a community, is the position or role of 'Lecturer', an appointment which dates from Elizabethan times. In the days before the Reformation, the main role of the parish priest was conducting services rather than preaching sermons. Preaching work would normally have been undertaken by a travelling friar from a nearby religious house or monastery, an activity which of course became redundant following their suppression by Henry VIII in the 1530s. During the years which followed these events, many communities, including that at Dedham, decided to hire the services of a town preacher or lecturer to do the job for them. These men were often university-trained academics with the knowledge and skills required for the effective preaching of God's word. At Dedham, the Lecturer's duties included taking the children for Sunday school and delivering a sermon to the congregation between 8–9 am on Tuesday mornings, prior to the start of the weekly wool market.

The bust of Lecturer John Rogers who is wearing a skull cap, ruff and gown. The Author

The first of the Dedham lecturers was a man called Edmund Chapman who held the position from about 1577 until his death in 1602. He was succeeded in 1605 by John Rogers, who became the most famous lecturer of them all. His style of preaching earned him the nickname 'Roaring Rogers' and crowds would flock from all over the district to hear him. Even undergraduates from Cambridge University are known to have made the journey across country on horseback to hear him speak. And speak he did. Roaring from the pulpit to the 1200-plus congregation, he would frequently have them 'deluged by their own tears' as he took them to task for not reading their bibles. In fact, such was his popularity, that it wasn't long before large galleries had to be erected across the western end of the church to accommodate the vast crowds. And at the time of his funeral thirty-one years later, these galleries were said to have nearly collapsed under the sheer weight of the mourners.

Although the galleries have long since disappeared, evidence of their existence can still be seen on some of the stone columns just inside the main door of the church. About ten feet up, you can see a mass of graffiti carved into the stone work – presumably the work of young

Visitors pause to admire John Constable's 1822 painting The Ascension *which hangs on the south wall of the church.* EADT

children as they sat up in the gallery whiling away their time during the long sermons. A high level opening cut into the wall of the south aisle opposite the main door to the church is another giveaway to there once being an upper story at this end of the building. In recent times, however, this opening has been covered with an original painting by John Constable. It is entitled *The Ascension* and was one of just three religious paintings completed by the artist during his career. It shows the risen Christ and was commissioned in 1822 by Edward Alston as an altarpiece for Manningtree church. There it remained until 1965, when it was acquired for All Saints' at Feering. In 1998, the painting was sold to raise funds for a new heating system and subsequently acquired by The Constable Trust for Dedham. In 2002, the painting was sent on loan to an exhibition of Constable's paintings at the Grand Palais in Paris.

The interior of the church contains numerous monuments dedicated to the great and the good of Dedham, some of whom are further remembered in the spacious churchyard outside. But of all the tombstones which adorn the churchyard, there is one which stands out as being a little unusual. It can be found standing hard up against the south wall of the church and at first glance could be mistaken for just a lump of old stone of little or no consequence. It is of irregular shape and stands about two feet high. But if one looks carefully at the front of the stone it is just possible to decipher the crudely written words, 'Edward Ward and Martha his Wife'. No date or further explanation is given and the identity of the couple has been the subject of numerous investigations over the years. One story has it that Edward Ward was a former ploughman of the parish, who was known for his blasphemous and irreligious behaviour. Apparently one day whilst he was ploughing the fields, and swearing away, a large stone or 'thunderbolt' fell from the sky right on top of him. When others arrived on the scene all that remained of him were his smouldering boots!

The roughly-hewn tombstone of Edward Ward against the south wall of the nave. The Author

Another, perhaps slightly more believable, explanation to the stone's existence was published in the local press in 1907. In this account, it stated that a ploughman, Edward Ward, employed on one of the local farms was one day following the tail of his plough across a field when he heard a sharp sound of the ploughshare hitting a mighty stone. Bringing his horses to a standstill, he uncovered the boulder and with great difficulty rolled it to the side of the field. He then became seized with the idea of having it for his tombstone when he departed this life and left careful instructions for his relatives to carry out his wishes. Whatever the truth of the matter, the stone will probably outlast all the other more traditional ancient monuments in the churchyard.

Directly opposite the church in the main street stands Sherman's Hall, a timber-framed building of c.1600 but with a most ornate brick frontage added around 1730. The house was originally built by Edmund Sherman, who subsequently bequeathed the building to the Governors of the Free Grammar School for use as a school to teach the village children how to 'read, write and cast accounts.' This was in contrast to the Latin and Greek dominated curriculum being taught at the Grammar School.

Several descendents of Edmund Sherman and other members of his family are known to have emigrated to America between the years 1633 and 1640. Their descendents include a co-founder of Rhode Island, a signatory of the Declaration of Independence and the famous W T Sherman of American Civil War fame. The result, of course, is that Dedham is particularly popular with American tourists, especially descendents of those who originated from the area.

Finally, a brief mention must be made of one other historic building in Dedham, which can be found just a short walk across the playing fields behind the church. It is known

Sherman's Hall – a former school for the village children. The Author

Southfields, a former medieval cloth factory. The Author

Time to relax by the river. The Author

as 'Southfields' and is thought to be the best-preserved example of a medieval cloth factory in the country. Dating in parts from the twelfth century, the building is of timber-frame construction and made up of various sections joined together around a quadrangle – a most unusual concept for business premises of the period. Whether or not the complex operated as a factory as we would understand the word, or was simply the business premises and warehousing of a succession of wealthy clothiers, is not known. It does, however, have Grade 1 listed building status and has, over the last fifty or so years, been fully restored by its modern owners.

Setting on Record a Village's Memories

When Jenny Kay of Fordham wrote a letter in the local parish magazine asking if anyone would be interested in helping to set up a local history group, she wasn't sure if she would get a response. In fact, she failed to receive a single reply, but having later received one or two encouraging comments from locals she decided to hold a meeting anyway and then waited with baited breath to see if anyone would bother to turn up. This was back in March 1997 and to Jenny's delight nineteen people attended the meeting with two more sending their apologies – and thus was born the Fordham Local History Society.

Like many Essex villages Fordham is steeped in history with evidence of habitation dating back to Neolithic times. Archaeological excavations have also uncovered finds to suggest that the Romans may also have owned property here. At the time of the Domesday survey in 1086, the manor of Fordham was inhabited by at least twenty-five tenants and their families, along with two horses, eight cattle, eighty sheep, twenty-five goats, ten pigs and six beehives – all of which were valued at £7. And for the last 900 or so years successive generations have made their home here. They have worked and re-worked the same fields, worshipped in the same church and no doubt shared a regular drink in one of the local hostelries. By 1870, the population of Fordham had risen to over 800 and the value of the parish had increased to nearly £5,000. The current population of the village is still around the 800 mark.

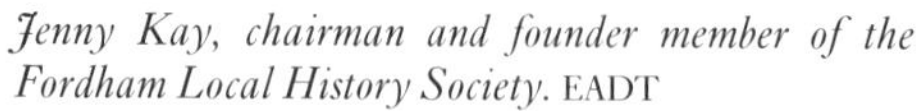

Jenny Kay, chairman and founder member of the Fordham Local History Society. EADT

Returning to the Fordham Local History Society, and to that inaugural meeting in

Members of the Fordham Local History Society. EADT

March 1997, a decision was made to form a proper group which would hold regular meetings and work together to record various aspects of the village's history. The group were fortunate in receiving help and advice from one or two seasoned researchers, including Pat Lewis who had been involved in researching her own Fordham ancestors for some years previously, as well as from numerous local residents who were willing to make available treasured family photographs and other information about village life. In fact, it was the compilation of a series of Fordham photographs, in the form of a book, that was to become the group's first major project.

Jenny recalls that this was very much a joint effort with help received from numerous people in the village, as well as from others with an interest in Fordham family history. It was three years before the book was finally published, but the end result was well worth the wait. The pictures span the years 1842–2000 and provide a nostalgic look back at life in the village over the last hundred or so years. It's all there – farm workers, school groups, Sunday school outings, villages fetes and a record of many local buildings, some of which no longer remain. To date, about 500 copies of the book have been sold and plans are in place for a second volume.

Spurred on by the success of their first project, the group has moved on to tackle a number of other initiatives. These include an attempt to complete a survey of all the old timber-framed buildings in the village with a view to measuring and preparing drawings of the structures, as well as learning about the people who once resided in them. Help in achieving this aim has come in the form of local timber-frame building expert Richard Shackle who has led the group on a number of site visits. Of particular interest was a visit to the *Shoulder of Mutton* public house, which is reputed to be the oldest inn in the village – it is certainly one of the oldest buildings dating from the fifteenth century, or perhaps even earlier. Although much altered over the years, in its original form it would have consisted of a central hall with two cross wings. The hall would have been open from the ground floor to the roof and the smoke from the central hearth would have filtered its way out through the adjacent windows and gaps in the roof. One of the cross wings (the low end) would have contained two service rooms (buttery and pantry), whilst the other wing would have contained the parlour (the high end). Both of the cross wings would have contained upper floors for sleeping arrangements. The earliest available licensing records show that the building was being used as an inn from at least 1769, and the name 'Shoulder of Mutton' was probably chosen as a symbol of the local farming community. Interestingly, there is also evidence that part of the building was being used a butcher's shop in the late Victorian period.

The Shoulder of Mutton *pub, 2004.* EADT

In the autumn of 2001, the group received a bit of a boost when Jess and Theresa Jephcott and the two sons Lewis and Harry moved into the village. Both Jess and Theresa are well known local history researchers and it didn't take them long to sign up as members for the Fordham Local History Society. In fact, Theresa has since become a member of the local parish council and Jess has become increasingly involved in the group's research activities. In particular, he has taken on the job of trying to research all the names which are inscribed on the village war memorial, as well as instigating a local oral history project.

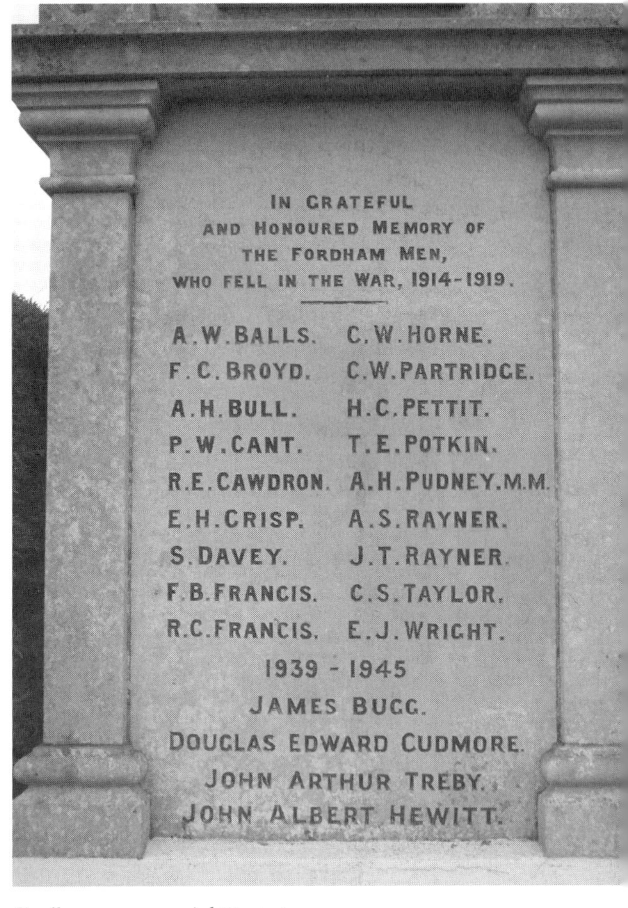

Fordham war memorial. The Author

Jess tells me that one of the best sources he has found for finding information on the names listed on the memorial has been the Commonwealth War Graves Commission's web site. This has provided details relating to the way in which the individuals concerned died and where they are buried. The 1901 census has also provided information on where the individuals were born and were living at the time of the survey. However, Jess would still like to uncover more details about the personal lives of the individuals concerned and, perhaps, find some photographs to add to the documentary record (see names on war memorial picture).

Perhaps the most interesting of the group's projects to date, however, and one that is sure to involve the wider community, is the launch of the 'Fordham Recalled' project. This is an attempt to record the memories of as many Fordham people as possible, and as noted above, is currently being spearheaded by Jess Jephcott. The idea to record the memories of local people came from a similar exercise which has been carried out in Colchester with great success for a number of years. However, unlike the basic tape recordings made by the Colchester group, the Fordham interviews are being recorded on film, which of course can only serve to enhance the material recovered.

Of the five people interviewed to date, the oldest has been Margaret (Girlie) Payle who was born in the village in 1908. Girlie had quite a lot to say about her early days in Fordham:

Society members Pat Lewis, Theresa Jephcott and Paul Doughhty examine old Fordham census records. Jess Jephcott

> We didn't have a bathroom until 1964. Our water came from a nearby brook and we had to fetch our drinking water in buckets from the nearby well. For Christmas, we didn't get much. We might get a sugar mouse, a sausage roll, mince pie, an apple or an orange in our stocking.

Speaking about local personalities, Girlie recalled the days when tramps would regularly visit the village, 'Tramps from the workhouse (later St Albrights) would pass through the village on their way to Sudbury', she recalled. 'They would call in for some hot water for their tins to make their tea. They were never any bother.'

Another person interviewed is Angela Church whose family moved to Fordham when she was about ten years old at the start of the Second World War. Speaking about the threat posed by the German doodlebugs in the later years of the war, Angela recalled lying in bed and listening to the drone of their engines as they passed overhead:

> I can remember being in bed during the middle of the night and I could hear what sounded like a two-stroke motorcycle. The dog was on the bed, something

Jess Jephcott interviews Marlene Boyle (Fordham resident and founder member of society). The Author

that wasn't normally allowed, and he was shaking like a jelly. Then this noise cut out and a short while later there was this almighty crash. By then I was sitting up comforting the dog and then a huge lump of plaster fell off the ceiling and landed on my pillow. If is wasn't for the dog it would have landed on me.

INDEX